General editor: Graham Hand

Brodie's Notes on Chaucer's

The Nun's Priest's Tale

Pan Books London, Sydney and Auckland

First published with parallel texts 1978 by Pan Books Ltd
This revised edition published 1986 by
Pan Books Ltd, Cavaye Place, London SW10 9PG
9 8 7 6 5 4 3
© Pan Books Ltd 1986
ISBN 0 330 50238 7
Photoset by Parker Typesetting Service, Leicester
Printed and bound in Great Britain by
Richard Clay (The Chaucer Press) Ltd, Bungay, Suffolk

Contents

Preface

This student revision aid is based on the principle that any close examination of Chaucer's text is essential to a full understanding of his artistry. He is by common agreement one of our greatest comic poets, and *The Canterbury Tales* is his masterpiece. But because his language is not easy to understand, some due attention must be given to it and the ways in which it differs from our language today. Consequently each editor of a parallel text Chaucer in this series will give an account of Chaucer's grammar, versification and pronunciation.

The full text of the *Tale* will be given on the left hand side of the page, and opposite this there will be a colloquial prose translation. This must not be regarded as a 'crib'. Students should read it carefully against the original, consulting the glossary and textual notes in order to arrive at a full understanding of the meaning and, one hopes, of the nature of Chaucer's art. That art will be examined by each editor, who will deal with Chaucer's characterization, his humour, his narrative skills, the images he uses, indeed any aspect of his work which merits critical attention and comment. And further, when one has learned to read Chaucer and appreciate him, some knowledge will be necessary of the age in which he lived, and his place in it if that appreciation is to be extended. There will be a brief account of Chaucer's life and times, and the student is advised to look carefully at the textual notes and the critical commentary mentioned above. Revision questions and general questions are also included, and there will be a guideline note-form answer to one of the questions. The aim is not merely to prepare the student thoroughly for an examination, but also to introduce him to the challenge and delight of Chaucer by involving him directly with the text. That text is its own reward, for both the *Prologue* and the *Tales* are among the greatest imaginative literature of all time.

Graham Handley

Literary terms used in these notes

Irony Irony is easier to detect in practice than it is to define. One broad definition would be that irony is the exploitation of the gap between the way things appear and the way they really are. In *The Nun's Priest's Tale*, Chauntecleer's vanity and his view of himself as a prince in a kingdom are, in part, ironic because we are aware that his environment is no more than a little farmyard. Most irony is unperceived by the person who is its 'victim'; for example, a figure in a novel or play might compliment himself or criticize others while we, as readers or audience, will be aware that the compliment is inappropriate (a coward might claim to be a brave man, like Falstaff in *Henry IV*) or that the criticism of others would be better applied to the speaker himself. This kind of irony involves a contradiction between words and actions. The term 'ironic' is also sometimes used to describe an unexpected turn or reversal of events in a narrative – in *The Nun's Priest's Tale* it is ironic that Chauntecleer wins his freedom from the fox by employing the same sort of cunning that the fox had first used against him.

Rhetoric In Chaucer's time, rhetoric formed one of the staple school subjects. It concerned itself with the rules governing literary composition, matters of structure and style. When Chaucer, in the person of the Nun's Priest, turns aside to address 'destiny' (line 572) or 'Venus' (576) he is following rhetorical practice in the way in which he invokes the abstract force or the goddess. Similarly, the list of 'examples' of people who have been forewarned by their dreams (344–382), provided by Chauntecleer, adheres to the rhetorical method of argument and debate.

Alliteration Words beginning with the same letter, as in

Of *b*ras they *b*roghten *b*emes, and of *b*ox

Onomatopeia Words or phrases which actually reflect the sounds of what is being described, as in the two lines which follow the one above:

Of horn, of boone in whiche they blewe and *powped*,
And therwithal they *shriked* and they *howped*;

A brief description of Chaucer's life and works

Geoffrey Chaucer was born about 1340 near the Tower of London. He was born into the age of Edward III, and of the Black Prince, into the Age of Chivalry and the magnificent court of Edward III with knights and ladies, heraldry and tournaments, minstrels and poetry, music and story-telling.

Chaucer entered into this rich and colourful courtly world at an early age, when he became a page in the household of the Countess of Ulster, wife to Lionel, later Duke of Clarence, and one of the sons of Edward III. This was clearly arranged by his parents, who had some contacts at Court. His mother's first husband had been Keeper of the King's Wardrobe, and there can be little doubt that she had something to do with the appointment of Chaucer's father as deputy to the King's Butler. The first record of Geoffrey Chaucer appears in an account book, dating from 1357, which records a payment by the royal household to a London tailor for a cloak, multi-coloured breeches and a pair of shoes for the young page Chaucer. It was in the Duke's great houses in London and Yorkshire that the young page would have learned the elegant and aristocratic code of manners, and made the acquaintance of the high and the noble. He would have learned French and Latin, the languages of the Court, the Church and the educated classes. It was also one of the duties of a page to play and sing, and to recite poetry.

The next record we have is that Chaucer was taken prisoner by the French in 1359, during one of the campaigns in The Hundred Years' War, and ransomed in the following year – the King himself contributing £16 (a very large sum in those days) of the money. So Chaucer must have seen active service in the French wars, probably as a squire attending on one of the nobles, like the squire in the *Canterbury Tales* who attended on the Knight, his father. For the upper classes, the experience of being a prisoner of war in the Age of Chivalry was not too uncomfortable. It was normal for the 'prisoner' to be entertained as a 'house guest' until the ransom was paid, and it is probable that during this enforced stay in France Chaucer became thoroughly versed in French literature, particularly the *Roman de la Rose* (the procedure manual, as it were, for 'courtly love'), which was to have such an important influence on his literary work.

After his ransom was paid, Chaucer returned to his Court duties, and soon in a more elevated position. He became one of the valets in attendance on the King. In 1366 his father died and his mother married again. It is probable that in the same year he married Philippa, daughter of Sir Payne Roet and sister of Katherine Swynford, the mistress and later third wife to John of Gaunt. Philippa was a lady-in-waiting to the Queen. As a valet to the King, Chaucer would carry candles 'before the King', tidy up his bedroom and attend to a variety of duties which were to become more and more concerned with affairs of state. In 1386 he was sent abroad on the official business of the Crown. About this time he was promoted from valet to palace official. It appears that Chaucer went soldiering again in 1369, probably on one of John of Gaunt's campaigns in Picardy. In 1370 he was abroad again on the King's service, and we can now see him becoming a trusted civil servant as he was frequently sent on missions to France, Flanders and Italy. During his visits to Italy on official business Chaucer took the opportunity to become familiar with Italian literature, most especially the works of Petrarch, Boccaccio and Dante, which were to influence much of his subsequent poetry.

In 1374 he was promoted to a senior position as Comptroller of Customs and Subsidy (for wool, skins and hides) at the Port of London, and the City of London bestowed on him the lease of a house in Aldgate.

From about 1380 Chaucer settled down to his life as senior customs official, as there is only one record of further journeys abroad. He must have been respected as a man of affairs, as he became a Justice of the Peace in 1385, and a Member of Parliament, or Knight of the Shire for Kent, soon afterwards.

It was during these years that Chaucer found time to write seriously. His early literary attempts were influenced considerably by French literature. Then, when John of Gaunt left the country in 1386 on an adventure to claim the crown of Castile, the King's uncle, the Duke of Gloucester, took charge of the country's affairs (Richard being not yet of age), and Chaucer suffered from the new influences in royal patronage. He lost his

Comptrollership of Customs, he was not re-elected to Parliament and he had to give up his house in Aldgate. We even learn that he felt himself in danger of being sued for debt. Chaucer had now plenty of time to ponder and at this time he must have been preparing *The Canterbury Tales*.

In 1389 a rumour was abroad that the great Duke of Lancaster (Chaucer's patron John of Gaunt) was returning home. This helped the young King Richard II in taking over the reins of power from his uncle Gloucester. It has been stated that the young King Richard knew Chaucer and liked his poetry. There must be some substance in this, as shortly afterwards Chaucer was appointed Clerk of the King's Works. John of Gaunt returned to England in November 1389, and for the rest of his life Chaucer was to enjoy royal patronage and a comfortable living. It was in these years of semi-retirement that *The Canterbury Tales* were written. Alas, Chaucer died without having finished his masterpiece. His tomb in Westminster Abbey gives the date of his death – October 1400.

It seems probable that 1387 was the approximate date of commencement for *The Canterbury Tales*. Chaucer's renown rests mainly on this work, but in terms of volume the *Tales* form less than half of his writing which has come down to us. Besides a number of shorter poems, there are five other major works in verse and two or three in prose. Chaucer's most important production during his first tentative years as a writer was the translation he probably made of the *Roman de la Rose*, the style and content of which was to have such a great influence on his writing. His first major poem was *The Book of the Duchess*, a poem steeped in the French tradition, written about 1370 to commemorate the death of Blanche, Duchess of Lancaster and wife of his patron, John of Gaunt. This was the first of four love-vision poems, the others being *The House of Fame, The Parliament of Fowls* and *The Legend of Good Women* (whose date is doubtful). Chaucer's works can be conveniently grouped into three parts, the French period, the Italian period and the English period; and, generally speaking, the periods follow one another in chronological sequence. The French period showed the influence of the *Roman de la Rose*, and included the love-vision poems. The Italian period (1380–5), marked by the narrative poem *Troilus and Criseyde*, rehandles a theme of the Italian poet Boccaccio. *Troilus and Criseyde* is a masterpiece, and is still considered to be the finest narrative poem in English, full of beauty and lyrical quality, and delightful humour in the character of Pandarus. The English period (1389–1400) is the last, and is the period when Chaucer reached his full maturity as a dramatic poet. This is the period of *The Canterbury Tales*, a collection of tales and tellers that is unique in English literature. Chaucer died before he could complete this great masterpiece.

It must be emphasized that these terms, 'French,' 'Italian', 'English' for Chaucer's literary life only indicate predominant influences: the stories in *The Canterbury Tales* are drawn from far and wide; *The Knight's Tale*, for instance, again owes its theme to a story by Boccaccio.

Setting and origin of the *Tale*

In *The Prologue to The Canterbury Tales* Chaucer tells us that he had already taken lodgings at the Tabard Inn, Southwark, in preparation to begin the next day his pilgrimage to the shrine of St Thomas à Becket at Canterbury Cathedral, when twenty-nine pilgrims appeared at the same inn. Chaucer is soon made one of their company. The inn-keeper, Harry Bailly, suggests that they should ease the tedium of the two days' journey to the shrine by telling stories on the way. The proposal is accepted; he is to be the judge; and the teller of the best story will receive a supper at the others' expense when they get back to the Tabard. The Host's original plan – and it was a very ambitious one from Chaucer's point of view – was that each traveller should tell two stories on the outward journey and two on the return.

After riding a mile or two from London on the following morning, the Host halts the company and arranges that the pilgrims, who in their occupations represent a cross-section of medieval society, draw lots to see who will begin the string of narratives. Appropriately, in view of his social status, the Knight is the one to whom the lot falls first. He is followed by the Miller and the Reeve. Several more tales have been told before the Monk is called upon. His story, concerning the downfall of famous men, so depresses the company that the Knight stops him and asks for something more cheerful, a request which is eagerly seconded by the Host, who then summons the Nun's Priest to give them a tale to 'gladden our hearts'. The Priest agrees, aware that he will be blamed if he does not come up with something in marked contrast to the Monk's gloomy lines. In fact, the relationship between the *Monk's Tale* and the *Nun's Priest's* is a mischievous one. The story of Chauntecleer, the cock who was almost destroyed by his own pride and vanity, reflects in a comical fashion on the Monk's list of men, such as Samson or Julius Caesar, who have been struck down in the midst of their prosperity. One or two references (for example, lines 438–43) indicate that this reflection is deliberate.

It is not easy to determine the origin of the story of the *Fox and the Cock*, but it is certain that Chaucer did not invent it. At one time, as the Nun's Priest reminds us, 'beestes and briddes koude speke and synge', and stories abound in many folklores in which animals have the gift of speech. A Latin version of this story was well known in France in the twelfth century, under the title of *Gallus et Vulpes, the Cock and the Fox*. A still earlier version also in Latin verse was composed in the eighth century by Ealhwine, or Alcuin, of York, an English ally of Charlemagne, in his educational work. A German form of the tale, *Reinhart Fuchs*, belongs to the twelfth century, while Marie of France, who lived at the court of our King Henry II, wrote in French verse her *Dou Coc et dou Werpil*. *The Roman de Renart*, a collection of satirical fables in which the Fox is shown with his hand against everyone else, belongs to the thirteenth century.

We cannot tell from which, if any, of these versions Chaucer derived his Nun's Priest's Tale, for each seems to have contributed something to the story Sir John told; but wherever he found his material, Chaucer's version bears the imprint of the personality of Chaucer himself. Its 626 lines contain much which is not found in any of the older versions, and at least two-thirds may be considered additions made by Chaucer. There are lines, scattered throughout the piece, which might well resemble the exhortations of a priest to his congregation; the long accounts of the dreams of various noted dreamers occupy nearly one-third of the whole tale, and these are not found in the early versions which have come down to us; the detailed descriptions of the hero and his consort, and the comments put into the hero's mouth, are Chaucer's own contribution to the whole. It has been calculated that Chaucer's additions amount to more than twice the amount he took from the extant versions he probably knew, and these additions are certainly in the poet's own manner.

Plot

The story told by the Nun's Priest is simple. In a farmyard, belonging to an old widow, live a cock, Chauntecleer, and seven hens. His 'favourite' among this retinue, and the only one to be named by the author, is Pertelote. Chauntecleer describes to Pertelote how he saw in a dream an animal 'like a hound' which intended to seize him. He claims almost to have died with fear of the beast's look. Pertelote mocks her 'husband' for his cowardice and his superstitious belief in dreams. Chauntecleer is inclined to put his trust in the prophetic power of dreams and recounts a couple of stories to support his point of view, but despite his conviction that he will suffer some misfortune because of the dream, he appears to forget about the warning he has received. The next day Chauntecleer is strutting about the yard when he sees a fox in the vegetable garden. By flattery, the fox gets the cock to sing and to close his eyes when doing so. The fox snatches the bird by the throat and runs off with him towards a wood. A human and animal pursuit follows. Chauntecleer tells the fox that now he has come safely to the edge of the wood he should proclaim to his pursuers his intention of eating the bird. The fox opens his mouth to speak and the cock escapes from his captor and takes refuge up a tree, from which he will not again be tempted by the fox. Both animals have learned a kind of lesson.

The Prologe of *The Nonnes Preestes Tale*

'Hoo!' quod the Knyght, 'good sire, namoore of this!
That ye han seyd is right ynough, y-wis,
And muchel moore; for litel hevynesse
Is right ynough to muche folk, I gesse.
I seye for me, it is a great disese,   5
Where as men han been in greet welthe and ese,
To heeren of hire sodeyn fal, allas!
And the contrarie is joye and greet solas,
As whan a man hath been in povre estaat,
And clymbeth up, and wexeth fortunat,   10
And there abideth in prosperitee:
Swich thyng is gladsom, as it thynketh me,
And of swich thyng were goodly for to telle.'

'Ye,' quod oure Hoost, 'by seinte Poules belle!
Ye seye right sooth. This Monk he clappeth lowde   15
He spak, how 'Fortune covered with a clowde'—
I noot nevere what – and also of a 'Tragedie'
(Right now ye herde), and pardee, no remedie
It is for to biwaille ne compleyne
That that is doon; and als it is a peyne,   20
As ye han seyd, to heere of hevynesse.

Sire Monk, namoore of this, so God yow blesse!
Youre tale anoyeth al this compaignye:
Swich talkyng is nat worth a boterflye,
For therinne is ther no desport ne game.   25
Wherfore sire Monk, daun Piers by youre name,
I pray yow hertely, telle us somwhat elles,
For sikerly, nere clynkyng of youre belles
That on youre bridel hange on every syde,
By hevene-kyng that for us alle dyde!   30
I sholde er this han fallen doun for sleep,
Althogh the slough had never been so deep;

The Prologue of *The Nun's Priest's Tale*

'Now then,' exclaimed the Knight, 'I beg you, let us have no more of this! What you have said is quite enough indeed, and much more than enough; for I think sadness in small doses is quite sufficient for many people. Honestly, speaking for myself, I find it rather wearisome to hear of the sudden fall of men who once enjoyed prosperity and comfort. On the other hand, it does give joy and satisfaction to hear that, when a person has lived in straitened circumstances, he is improving his lot and is getting better fortune and, ultimately, maintains a prosperous state. Such a case, it seems to me, is a cheerful one and stories of such circumstances are good to relate.'

'Yes,' our Host replied, 'by St Paul's great bell, what you say is true. This Monk here has been chattering noisily and saying how "Fortune has had a fall" or something to that effect – I think it was a tragedy of sorts – anyhow you heard it just now – and, on my word, bewailing or complaining about something that is gone and done with will not put things right. As you yourself have remarked, it is far from comforting to hear stories of sorrow.

Now, sir Monk, may God bless you but let us have no more of this talk. Your tale has put our whole company on edge. Indeed, as there is neither amusement nor humour in such stories, they are not worth a butterfly.

And so, Sir Monk – Lord Piers, that's your name, so I hear – I heartily beg of you to tell us some other story, for surely, were it not for the jingling of the bells hanging from the sides of your bridle, I swear by the King of Heaven who died for us I should have fallen off to sleep long ago, in spite of the depth of the mud on the road.

Thanne hadde youre tale al be toold in veyn:
For, certeinly, as that thise clerkes seyn,
Where as a man may have noon audience,   35
Noght helpeth it to tellen his sentence.
And wel I woot the substance is in me,
If any thyng shal wel reported be:
Sire, sey somwhat of huntyng, I yow preye.'
   'Nay,' quod this Monk, 'I have no lust to pleye;   40
Now lat another telle, as I have toold.'

   Thanne spak oure Hoost, with rude speche and boold,
And seyde unto the Nonnes Preest anon,
'Com neer, thou preest, com hyder thou, sir John;
Telle us swich thyng as may oure hertes glade;   45
Be blithe, though thou ryde upon a jade;
What thogh thyn hors be bothe foul and lene?
If he wol serve thee, rekke nat a bene;
Looke that thyn herte be murie evermo.'

   'Yis sire,' quod he, 'yis, Hoost, so moot I go!   50
But I be myrie, y-wis I wol be blamed.'
And right anon his tale he hath attamed,
And thus he seyde unto us everichon,
This sweete preest, this goodly man, sir John.

What is more, if that had actually happened, your story would have been told to no purpose, for I hardly need remind you what the scholars say, "It is useless for a person to speak if he cannot get a hearing." I know only too well that I have the makings of a good listener if a story is well told; so please tell us some hunting exploit, sir.'

'No,' answered the monk, 'I take no delight in frivolity. I have told my story, so let someone else tell one.'

Our Host then said some harsh, bold remarks but soon addressed the Nun's Priest, 'Come nearer, my priest; come this way, Sir John, and tell us a story to cheer us up. Still, be cheerful, even though your mount is only a hack. What does it matter if your horse is dirty and thin? As long as he serves your purpose, you should not care a bean. Come on, see that you are more cheerful from now on.'

'Yes, sir,' the Nun's Priest said, 'yes, Sir host, that is just what I must do. If I do not cheer up, by Heavens, you may well blame me.' Straightaway his story was started and this is what this amiable priest, this excellent man, Sir John, told all of us.

The Nun's Priest's Tale

A Poure wydwe, somdel stape in age,   55
Was whilom dwellyng in a narwe cotage,
Beside a greve, stondynge in a dale.
This wydwe, of which I telle yow my tale,
Syn thilke day that she was last a wyf
In paciënce ladde a ful symple lyf,   60
For litel was hir catel and hir rente;
By housbondrie of swich as God hire sente
She fond hirself and eek hire doghtren two.
Thre large sowes hadde she, and namo;
Three kyn, and eek a sheep that highte Malle.   65

Ful sooty was hir bour, and eek hire halle,
In which she eet ful many a sklendre meel;
Of poynaunt sauce hir neded never a deel;
No deyntee morsel passed thurgh hir throte,
Hir diete was accordant to hir cote;   70
Repleccioun ne made hire never sik;
Attempree diete was al hir phisik,
And exercise, and hertes suffisaunce.

The goute lette hire no-thyng for to daunce,
Napoplexië shente nat hir heed;   75
No wyn ne drank she, neither whit ne reed;
Hir bord was served moost with whit and blak,
Milk and broun breed, in which she fond no lak,
Seynd bacoun and somtyme an ey or tweye;
For she was, as it were, a maner deye.   80
A yeerd she hadde, enclosed al aboute
With stikkes and a drye dych withoute,
In which she hadde a cok, heet Chauntecleer;
In al the land of crowyng nas his peer.

The Nun's Priest's Tale

Here begins The Nun's Priest's Tale of the Cock and Hen, Chaunte-cleer and Pertelote.

Once upon a time there was a poor widow, quite advanced in years, who dwelt in a small cottage in a grove situated in a dale. Since the death of her husband, this widow about whom my story is concerned had patiently lived a simple life, for her property and income were scanty. By means of careful management of the commodities that God sent her, however, she provided for herself and her two daughters. All she owned were three large sows, three cows and also a sheep called Molly.

Her bedroom and living-room, where she ate her scanty meals, were stained with soot and, although she never lacked spicy sauce, she never ate any delicious titbit, for her diet was much in keeping with the state of her cottage. She was never sick from overeating, as she found her moderate diet acted like medicine and exercise to her and provided her heart with contentment.

Gout in no way prevented her from dancing nor was her head harmed by apoplexy. She drank neither white nor red wine. Her table was usually provided with simple fare, milk and brown bread, of which she had plenty, broiled bacon and sometimes an egg or two, for she was, as it were, a kind of dairy-woman of sorts.

She owned a yard, enclosed by a fence with a dry ditch around it, where she kept a cock, called Chantecleer, who had no equal through-out the countryside in crowing.

His voys was murier than the murie orgon   85
On messe-dayes that in the chirche gon;
Wel sikerer was his crowyng in his logge
Than is a clokke or an abbey orlogge:
By nature he knew eche ascencioun
Of the equynoxial in thilke toun;   90
For whan degrees fiftene weren ascended,
Thanne crew he that it myghte nat been amended.
His coomb was redder than the fyn coral,
And batailled, as it were a castel wal;
His byle was blak, and as the jeet it shoon;   95
Lyk asure were his legges and his toon;
His nayles whiter than the lylye flour,
And lyk the burned gold was his colour.

   This gentil cok hadde in his governaunce
Sevene hennes for to doon al his pleasaunce,   100
Whiche were his sustres and his paramours,
And wonder lyk to hym as of colours;
Of whiche the faireste hewed on hir throte
Was cleped faire damoysele Pertelote.
Curteys she was, discreet and debonaire   105
And compaignable; and bar hyrself so faire
Syn thilke day that she was seven night oold,
That trewely she hath the herte in hoold
Of Chauntecleer, loken in every lith;
He loved hire so that wel was hym therwith.   110

But swiche a joye was it to here hem synge,
Whan that the brighte sonne gan to sprynge,
In sweete accord, 'My lief is faren in londe.'
For thilke tyme, as I have understonde,
Beestes and briddes koude speke and synge.   115
   And so bifel that in the dawenynge,
As Chauntecleer among his wyves alle
Sat on his perche that was in the halle,
And next hym sat this faire Pertelote,
This Chauntecleer gan gronen in his throte,   120
As man that in his dreem is drecched soore.

He's a cockerell though!

Indeed, his crowing had a more cheerful note than the joyous music that is played in churches on festival days and, what is more, when he crowed on his roost, it was more regular than a clock, even the great abbey clock. Moreover, he must have known every degree of celestial longitude on the celestial equator as judged in that village; for when the equinoctial had moved round fifteen degrees, no one could better him in his fine crowing. His comb, redder than fine coral, was crenellated like a castle wall, his black bill shone like jet, his legs and toes were of sky-blue colour with nails whiter than the lily; and his plumage was coloured like burnished gold.

To satisfy his personal pleasure this noble cock kept seven hens who were his sisters and lovers and who were amazingly like him in colour. The most beautiful of them, called sweet Miss Pertelote, had a brightly-coloured breast. She was so courteous, discreet, gracious and sociable and had conducted herself so becomingly, ever since she was a week old, that she had completely won the heart of Chantecleer; and he was totally in her power. He was madly in love with her and was very pleased with himself about the affair.

I tell you it was delightful to hear them both sing 'My beloved has gone away' in close harmony when the brilliant sun sprang up; for birds and animals could, so I understand, speak and sing at that time.

One dawn, as Chantecleer was sitting on his perch in the living-room with all his wives, beautiful Pertelote sitting next to him, it so happened that he made queer noises in his throat just like a man who is sore troubled in his dream.

And whan that Pertelote thus herde hym roore,
She was agast and seyde, 'O herte deere!
What eyleth yow, to grone in this manere?
Ye been a verray sleper; fy, for shame!' 125
    And he answerde and seyde thus: 'Madame,
I pray yow that ye take it nat agrief;
By God, me mette I was in swich meschief
Right now, that yet myn herte is soore afright.
Now God,' quod he, 'my swevene recche aright, 130
And kepe my body out of foul prisoun.
Me mette how that I romed up and doun
Withinne our yeerd, wheer-as I saugh a beest
Was lyk an hound, and wolde han maad areest
Upon my body and han had me deed. 135

His colour was bitwixe yelow and reed,
And tipped was his tayl and bothe his eeris
With blak, unlyk the remenant of his heeris;
His snowte smal, with glowynge eyen tweye:
Yet of his look for feere almoost I deye; 140
This caused me my gronyng douteless.'
    'Avoy!' quod she, 'fy on yow, hertelees!
Allas!' quod she, 'for by that God above
Now han ye lost myn herte and al my love;

I kan nat love a coward, by my feith; 145
For certes, what so any womman seith,
We alle desiren, if it myghte bee,
To han housbondes hardy, wise and free,
And secree, and no nygard, ne no fool,
Ne hym that is agast of every tool, 150
Ne noon avauntour. By that God above,
How dorste ye seyn, for shame, unto youre love
That any thyng myghte make yow aferd?
Have ye no mannes herte, and han a berd?
Allas! and konne ye been agast of swevenys? 155

When Pertelote heard him making these queer noises, she was frightened and said, 'O my dear sweetheart, what is your trouble to make you groan like this? You are acting like a deep sleeper! Fie on you! For shame!'

'Madam,' he answered her, 'please do not take it amiss. By God, I dreamt that I was in such trouble just now that my heart is deeply scared. Now, please God,' he went on, 'let my dream turn out well and keep my body from that foul prison! I dreamt that, as I was roaming up and down in our yard, I saw a beast like a hound which wanted to seize my body forcibly and kill me.

His colour was a mixture of yellow and red, his tail and ears, unlike the rest of his coat, were both trimmed with black, his snout was small and his two eyes glared – but even now I am almost dying with fear from the mere memory of his appearance. I can assure you it was this which caused my groaning.'

'What!' Pertelote exclaimed. 'Shame on you, you coward! By Heavens and by God above you have now lost the love of my whole heart.

I swear I cannot love a coward. Let me tell you, whatever they may say, all women desire to have, if possible, husbands who are bold, wise, generous and discreet, not a miser or a spendthrift, nor one who is afraid of every weapon or one who is a braggart. By God above, how dare you make such a shameful statement to your loved one that anything can scare you? Don't you possess the heart, or even the beard, of a man? Alas! Can you be so afraid of dreams?

No thyng, God woot, but vanitee in swevene is.
Swevenes engendren of replecciouns,
And ofte of fume, and of complecciouns,
Whan humours been to habundant in a wight.
Certes this dreem, which ye han met to-nyght, 160
Cometh of the greet superfluytee
Of youre rede colera, pardee,
Which causeth folk to dreden in hir dremes
Of arwes, and of fyre with rede lemes,
Of rede beestes, that they wol hem byte, 165
Of contekes and of whelpes, grete and lyte;
Right as the humour of malencolye
Causeth ful many a man in sleepe to crye
For feere of blake beres or boles blake,
Or elles blake develes wole hem take. 170

Of othere humours koude I telle also
That werken many a man in sleepe ful wo;
But I wol passe as lightly as I kan.
Lo, Catoun, which that was so wys a man,
Seyde he nat thus, "Ne do no fors of dremes"? 175
    'Now, sire,' quod she, 'whan we flee fro the bemes,
For Goddes love as taak som laxatyf.
Up peril of my soule and of my lyf
I conseille yow the beste, I wol nat lye,
That bothe of colere and of malencolye 180
Ye purge yow; and, for ye shal nat tarie,
Though in this toun is noon apothecarie,
I shall myself to herbes techen yow
That shul been for youre hele and for youre prow;

And in oure yeerd tho herbes shall I fynde, 185
The whiche han of hire propretee by kynde
To purge yow bynethe and eek above.
Forget nat this for Goddes owene love,
Ye been ful coleryk of compleccioun;
Ware the sonne in his ascencioun 190
Ne fynde yow nat repleet of humours hoote;

God knows, they are empty things, for only vanity can find a place in dreaming. Dreams are the result of overeating and are often caused by vapours and excessive humours in a person. Surely, by Heavens, this dream you dreamt last night arose from great excess of bile which often causes people in their dreams to fear arrows and red flames of fire, red animals that wish to harm them, quarrels, huge and small dogs. In the same way the melancholy humour causes many men to cry out in their sleep for fear that black bears, black bulls or even that black devils will seize them.

I could also tell you about many other humours that cause trouble for many people in their sleep; but I shall dismiss them as lightly as possible. Take Cato who was such a wise man. Didn't he say, "Pay no heed to dreams."

'Now, sir,' she continued, 'when we fly down from these perches, for the love of God just take a little laxative. Out of sheer fear for the safety of my soul and my life, I am offering you the soundest advice – and there is no need for me to tell untruths. You should purge yourself of both your anger and melancholy. Since you should not delay and because there is no chemist in this town, I myself shall instruct you in the use of herbs that will act for your own good and benefit.

I shall find in our garden the herbs which possess, from their natural properties, the power both to purge you and make you vomit. For God's own love, don't forget this! You are very bilious in temperament, so be careful of the sun in the forenoon and don't let yourself be found with hot humours.

And if it do, I dar wel leye a grote
That ye shul have a fevere terciane
Or an agu, that may be youre bane.
A day or two ye shul have digestyves   195
Of wormes, er ye take youre laxatyves
Of lawriol, centaure and fumetere,
Or elles of ellebor that groweth there,
Of katapuce or of gaitrys beryis,
Of herbe-yve growyng in oure yeerd, that mery is;   200
Pekke hem up right as they growe and ete hem yn.
Be myrie, housbonde, for youre fader kyn;
Dredeth no dreem; I kan sey yow namoore.'

    'Madame,' quod he, 'graunt mercy of youre loore.
But nathelees as touchyng daun Catoun,   205
That hath of wysdom swich a greet renoun,
Though that he bad no dremes for to drede,
By God, men may in olde bookes rede
Of many a man, moore of auctorite
Than ever Catoun was, so moot I thee,   210
That al the revers seyn of his sentence,
And han wel founded by experience
That dremes been significaciouns
As wel of joye as of tribulaciouns,
That folk enduren in this lif present.   215
Ther nedeth make of this noon argument,
The verray preeve sheweth it in dede.

    Oon of the gretteste auctours that men rede
Seith thus, that whilom two felawes wente
On pilgrimage in a ful good entente,   220
And happed so they coomen in a toun,
Wher-as ther was swich congregacioun
Of peple, and eek so streit of herbergage,
That they ne founde as muche as o cotage
In which they bothe myghte y-logged bee,   225
Wherfore they mosten of necessitee
As for that nyght departen compaignye;
And ech of hem gooth to his hostelrye,
And took his loggyng as it wolde falle.

If you do, I am willing to wager a groat that you will suffer from a fever with fits every other day or even an ague that will be the death of you. For a day or two you must take digestive aids consisting of worms before you are dosed with laxatives of spurge laurel, lesser centaury, fumitory or else black hellebore that grows in the yard, caper spurge of buckthorn berries, crowfoot that also grows in our yard where it is very pleasant. Peck at them where they grow, and swallow them all up. For the sake of your family cheer up, my husband. I can only advise you not to be afraid of dreams.'

'Madam,' he answered, 'Thank you for the information but still, although Lord Cato who was so renowned for his wisdom advised us not to fear dreams, by God, anyone can read in ancient books about many people of greater influence than Cato who, by my hope to have a thriving life, stated the contrary to what he thought. Moreover, these views are firmly established on experience, namely that dreams are the portents both of joy and tribulations that people are suffering even now in this life. There is no point in arguing about it as the matter can be tested in books which prove it.

One of the greatest authors read by man says that two people once made a pilgrimage with the best of intentions. It so happened that they arrived at a town where there was such a very great crowd of people and such a shortage of accommodation that they could not find as much as a cottage where they could stay. They had, from necessity, to separate company for the night and each of them went to a separate lodging and took what accommodation he could get.

That oon of hem was logged in a stalle   230
Fer in a yeerd with oxen of the plough;
That oother man was logged wel ynough,
As was his aventure or his fortune,
That us governeth alle as in commune.
    And so bifel that, longe er it were day,   235
This man mette in his bed, ther-as he lay,
How that his felawe gan upon hym calle
And seyde, 'Allas! for in an oxes stalle
This nyght I shal be mordred ther I lye;
Now helpe me, deere brother, or I dye;   240
In alle haste com to me,' he seyde.
This man out of his sleepe for feere abrayde;
But whan that he was wakened of his sleepe,
He turned hym and took of this no keepe;
Hym thoughte his dreem nas but a vanitee.   245

Thus twies in his slepyng dremed hee,
And atte thridde tyme yet his felawe
Cam, as hym thoughte, and seide, 'I am now slawe:
Bihoold my bloody woundes, depe and wyde.
Arys up erly in the morwe tyde,   250
And at the west gate of the toun,' quod he,
'A carte ful of donge ther shaltow se,
In which my body is hid ful prively;
Do thilke carte arresten boldely.
My gold caused my mordre, sooth to sayn.'   255
And tolde hym every point how he was slayn,
With a ful pitous face pale of hewe.

And truste wel, his dreem he fond ful trewe;
For on the morwe, as soone as it was day,
To his felawes in he took the way,   260
And whan that he cam to his oxes stalle,
After his felawe he bigan to calle.
    The hostiler answerde hym anon
And seyde, 'Sire, your felawe is agon;
As soone as day he wente out of the toun.'   265

One of them stayed in a stable some distance from the farmyard and put up among the plough oxen; the other, through luck or fortune which rules all of us, was fairly comfortably accommodated.

It so happened that, long before day dawned, this person, as he lay in his bed, dreamt how his companion called upon him, "Help! I shall be murdered tonight when I am lying in this cowshed! Help me, dear brother, or I shall die. Come to me quickly!" he cried. His companion started up with fear from his sleep; but, after he awoke, thinking that his dream was a mere fancy, he turned over and bothered no more about it.

Twice in his sleep he had the same dream and, on the third occasion, he thought his companion said to him, "I am now dead! Look at my blood-stained wounds, deep and huge. Get up early tomorrow morning and you will find at the west gate of the town a cart full of dung, in which my body is cunningly hidden. Stop that cart! To tell you the truth, they murdered me to get my money." With a sad, deathly-pale expression he described to him exactly how he had been killed.

And you can take it from me that he found the dream was completely true; for, on the next day, as soon as it was day, he made his way to his companion's lodging and, when he arrived at the cow-shed, he began to shout for his companion.

The owner of the place told him at once, "Sir, your friend has left. He left the town at daybreak."

This man gan fallen in suspecioun,
Remembrynge on his dremes that he mette,
And forth he gooth, no lenger wolde he lette,
Unto the west gate of the toun, and fond
A dong carte, as it were to donge lond,   270
That was arrayed in that same wise
As ye han herd the dede man devyse;
And with an hardy herte he gan to crye
Vengeance and justice of this felonye.
'My felawe mordred is this same nyght,   275
And in this carte heere lith gapyng upright.
I cry out on the ministres,' quod he,
'That sholden kepe and reulen this citee;
Harrow! allas! heere lith my felawe slayn.'

What sholde I moore unto this tale sayn?   280
The people out sterte and caste the cart to grounde,
And in the myddel of the dong they founde
The dede man, that mordered was al newe.
    O blisful God, that art so just and trewe,
Lo! how that thou biwreyest mordre alway.   285
Mordre wol out, that se we day by day;
Mordre is so wlatsom and abhomynable
To God, that is so just and resonable,
That he ne wol nat suffre it heled be,
Though it abyde a yeer or two or thre;   290
Mordre wol out, this my conclusioun.

And right anon ministres of that toun
Han hent the carter and so soore hym pyned,
And eek the hostiler so soore engyned,
That they biknewe hire wikkednesse anon,   295
And were an-hanged by the nekke bon.

The companion, remembering his dreams, became suspicious and went immediately to the west gate of the town where he found a cart of dung being driven to the manure heap; and every detail was exactly as you have heard the dead man describe. With a bold spirit he began to call for vengeance and justice for this crime. "My companion has been murdered this very night and lies on his back in this cart with his mouth open! I must call for the magistrates," he said, "who should keep law and order in this town. Help! Help! My friend is lying here, slain!"

What need I add to this story? The people rushed out and, overturning the cart, found in the middle of the dung the body of the man who had been recently murdered.

O blessed God, who is so just and true! It is wonderful how you always reveal all murders! Daily we see that murder will out; murder is so monstrous and abominable in the eyes of God who is so just and guided by reason that he will not suffer it to be hidden, even though one, two or even three years should elapse. I am fully convinced that murder will be discovered.

The magistrates of that town at once arrested the carter and tortured him severely; further, the owner of the place was so racked that they confessed their crime immediately and were hanged by the neck.

Heere may men seen that dremes been to drede;
And certes in the same book I rede
Right in the nexte chapitre after this
(I gabbe nat, so have I joye or blis),   300
Two men that wolde han passed over see
For certeyn cause into a fer contree,
If that the wynd ne hadde been contrarie,
That made hem in a citee for to tarie
That stood ful myrie upon an haven syde;   305
But on a day agayn the even-tyde
The wynd gan chaunge, and blew right as hem leste.
Jolif and glad they wente unto his reste,
And casten hem ful erly for to saille.

But to that o man fil a greet mervaille;   310
That oon of him in slepyng as he lay,
Hym mette a wonder dreem agayn the day:
Him thoughte a man stood by his beddes syde
And hym comanded that he sholde abyde,
And seyde hym thus: "If thou tomorwe wende,   315
Thou shalt be dreynt, my tale is at an ende."
He wook and tolde his felawe what he mette,
And preyde hym his viage for to lette;
As for that day he preyde hym to byde.
His felawe, that lay by his beddes syde,   320
Gan for to laughe, and scorned him full faste;

"No dreem," quod he, "may so myn herte agaste,
That I wol lette for to do my thynges;
I sette not a straw by thy dremynges,
For swevenes been but vanytees and japes;   325
Men dreme al day of owles or of apes,
And of many a maze therwithal;
Men dreme of thyng that never was ne shal;
But sith I see that thou wolt heere abyde,
And thus forslewthen wilfully thy tyde,   330
God woot it reweth me, and have good day."

From this alone you can see that dreams must be feared. Again, I read in the same book, even in the very next chapter, – and by my hope to enjoy happy bliss, I am not deceiving you – how two men wanted, for some reason or other, to make a sea-voyage to a distant country. As the winds had been unfavourable, they were compelled to abide a time in a town situated in a delightful position on the side of the harbour. One day, about evening time, the wind changed and blew in the direction they desired. They retired to bed happy and contented, prepared to set sail early the next day.

Now listen. An amazing thing happened to one of those two. As he lay sleeping, before the dawn he had a wonderful dream. He imagined that a man stood by his bedside, commanding him to remain in that place and saying, "If you sail tomorrow, you will be drowned. That's my message to you." When he awoke, he related what he had dreamt to his companion and begged him to delay his sea-voyage, imploring him to stay there that day. His companion, lying on the side of his bed, began to laugh and make great fun of him.

"No dream," he said, "can so terrify me as to cause me to delay my business. I don't care a straw about your dreams. Dreams are merely fancies and delusions. People are forever dreaming about owls and apes and all kinds of bewildering things. Indeed, people dream about things that have never taken place and never shall take place. But I see you are fully decided to remain here and deliberately waste your time in sloth so, although I am sorry about it, God knows, I give you my compliments."

And thus he took his leve, and wente his way;
But er that he hadde half his cours y-seyled,
Noot I nat why ne what myschaunce it eyled,
But casuelly the shippes botme rente, 335
And shipe and man under the water wente
In sighte of othere shippes it bisyde,
That with hem seyled at the same tyde.
And therfore, faire Pertelote so deere,
By swiche ensamples olde yet maistow leere, 340
That no man sholde been to recchelees
Of dremes, for I seye thee doutelees
That many a dreem ful soore is for to drede.

Lo! in the lyf of Seint Kenelm I rede,
That was Kenulphus sone, the noble kyng 345
Of Mercenrike, how Kenelm mette a thyng.
A lite er he was mordred, on a day
His mordre in his avysioun he say.
His norice hym expowned every deel
His swevene, and bad hym for to kepe hym weel 350
For traisoun; but he nas but seven yeer oold,
And therfore litel tale hath he toold
Of any dreem, so hooly was his herte.
By God, I hadde levere than my sherte
That ye hadde rad his legende, as have I. 355

Dame Pertelote, I sey yow trewely,
Marcrobeus, that writ the Avisioun
In Affrike of the worthy Cipioun,
Affermeth dremes and seith that they been
Warnynge of thynges that men after seen; 360
And forther-moore I pray yow looketh wel,
In the Olde Testament, of Daniel,
If he heeld dremes any vanitee.
Reed eek of Joseph, and ther shul ye see
Wher dremes be somtyme – I sey nat alle – 365
Warnynge of thynges that shul after falle.
Looke of Egipte the kyng, daun Pharao,
His baker and his butiller also,
Wher they ne felte noon effect in dremes.

might withdrawn here.

In this way he took his leave and went on his way; but, before he had completed his voyage, I don't know what caused it or what misfortune befell him but, by some chance, the ship's bottom was torn away and both the crew and the ship went down in full view of the other ships, which had sailed at the same time as they. And so, my dear Pertelote, from such old stories you can learn that no one can be too negligent of his dreams, for I can confidently assure you that many dreams are to be greatly feared.

Again, I have read in the "Life of St Kenelm," the son of Kenulphus, the noble King of Mercia, how Kenelm had a dream a short time before he was murdered, actually seeing his own murder in his dream. Although his nurse explained every detail of his dream to him and bade him beware of treachery as a result, he paid little heed to any dream as he was hardly seven years old and possessed a pious nature as well. By God, rather than own a stitch of clothing, I wish that you had read the story, as I have.

Lady Pertelote, I am telling you the truth that Macrobeus, who recorded the vision of the noble Scipio in Africa, supports the value of dreams and maintains that they are the forerunners of events that people will experience later. Again, I beg of you to refer to the Old Testament in the portion concerning Daniel and see if he considered dreams to be unreal. Read also about Joseph and there you will see if dreams are not sometimes, mark I do not say always, the warning of things to come about. Refer again to Lord Pharaoh, the King of Egypt, to see if his baker and butler did not experience the consequences of dreams!

Whoso wol seken actes of sondry remes 370
May rede of dremes many a wonder thyng.
Lo! Cresus, which that was of Lyde kyng,
Mette he nat that he sat upon a tree,
Which signified he sholde anhanged bee?
Lo! heere Andromacha, Ectores wyf, 375
That day that Ector sholde lese his lyf,
She dremed on the same nyght biforn
How that the lyf of Ector sholde be lorn,
If thilke day he wente into bataille;
She warned hym, but it myghte nat availle; 380
He wente for to fighte natheles,
But he was slayn anon of Achilles.
But thilke tale is al to longe to telle,
And eek it is ny day, I may nat dwelle;

Shortly I seye as for conclusioun, 385
That I shal han of this avisioun
Adversitee; and I seye forthermoor,
That I ne telle of laxatyves no stoor,
For they been venymes, I woot it weel;
I hem diffye, I love hem never a deel. 390
Not let us speke of myrthe and stynte al this;
Madame Pertelote, so have I blis,
Of o thyng God hath sent me large grace;

For, whan I se the beautee of youre face,
Ye been so scarlet reed aboute youre eyen, 395
It maketh al my drede for to dyen,
For, al-so siker as *In principio*,
Mulier est hominis confusio —
Madame, the sentence of this Latyn is,
"Womman is mannes joye and al his blis"; 400
For, whan I feele a-nyght your softe syde,
Al-be-it that I may nat on yow ryde,
For that oure perche is maad so narwe, allas!
I am so ful of joye and of solas,
That I diffye bothe swevene and dreem.'

Anyone who reads the chronicles of different realms will find many wonderful things concerning dreams. Take the example of Croesus, the King of Lydia. Did he not dream that he was sitting upon a tree, thereby warning him that he would be hanged? Take, again, Andromache, the wife of Hector. On the very night that Hector was destined to lose his life, she had dreamt the previous night that his life would be lost if he went into battle. Her warning was of no avail, as he still went out to fight and he was killed at once by Achilles – but that is too long a story for me to relate. Day is at hand so I cannot stay here.

In a few words, I shall reap trouble from this dream of mine. What's more, I have no faith in laxatives for I know only too well they are poisonous. I defy them! I don't like them at all! Now let us talk of something cheerful and stop all this. Madam Pertelote, let us enjoy ourselves. God has much favoured me with one thing.

When I look at the beauty of your face, so scarlet-red around the eyes, it causes all my fear to die away. There is no doubt but that *In principio, mulier est hominis confusio* – Madam, the meaning of this Latin is, "Woman is man's whole joyful bliss!" When I feel your soft side near me at night-time, even though I may not mount you, because, sadly, our perch is so narrow, I am so full of joy and comfort that I am prepared then to defy both visions and dreams.'

And with that word he fley doun from the beem,
For it was day, and eke his hennes alle;
And with a chuk he gan hem for to calle,
For he hadde founde a corn, lay in the yerd.
Real he was, he was namoore aferd;   410
He fethered Pertelote twenty tyme,
And trad as ofte, er that it was pryme.
He looketh as it were a grym leoun,
And on his toos he rometh up and doun;
Hym deigned nat to sette his foot to grounde.   415
He chukketh whan he hath a corn y-founde,
And to hym rennen thanne his wyves alle.
Thus roial as a prince is in an halle
Leve I this Chauntecleer in his pasture,
And after wol I telle his aventure.   420

   Whan that the monthe in which the world bigan,
That highte March, whan God first maked man,
Was compleet, and passed were also,
Syn March bigan, thritty dayes and two,
Bifel that Chauntecleer in al his pryde,   425
His sevene wyves walkynge by his syde,
Caste up his eyen to the brighte sonne
That in the signe of Taurus hadde y-ronne
Twenty degrees and oon and som-what moore,
And knew by kynde and by noon oother loore   430
That it was pryme, and crew with blisful stevene.

'The sonne,' he seyde, 'is clomben up on hevene
Fourty degrees and oon and moore y-wis.
Madame Pertelote, my worldes blis,
Herkneth thise blisful briddes how they synge,   435
And se the fresshe floures how they sprynge;
Ful is myn herte of revel and solas.'
But sodeynly hym fil a sorweful cas;
For ever the latter ende of joy is wo;
God woot that worldly joye is soone ago;   440
And if a rethor koude faire endite,
He in a cronycle saufly myghte it write,
As for a sovereyn notabilitee.

With that, as day had now dawned, he flew with all his hens down from the beam and, clucking furiously, began to call for them, as he had discovered some corn lying in the yard. Having by now regained his regal aspect and being no longer afraid he stroked Pertelote twenty times and copulated with her as often, before nine in the morning. He looked like a fierce lion as he roamed on his toes about the place, disdaining to lay his foot on the ground and clucking so much when he found some corn that all his wives ran after him. I shall now leave Chantecleer feeding like this, as royal as a prince in his own hall, and I shall tell you later what happened to him.

When the month that is called March, the month when the world began and when God created Man, was over, and fully thirty-two days were passed since the end of that month, it so happened that Chantecleer, with his seven wives strutting alongside him, looked very proudly at the bright sun which was twenty-one degrees and probably more in the sign of Taurus. He knew by instinct, and not from any learning, that it was nine in the morning and so he sang with a cheerful note.

'The sun,' he said, 'has climbed forty-one degrees and, perhaps, more in the sky. Madam Pertelote, the delight of my life, listen to these happy birds singing and look how these fresh flowers are growing! My heart is full of joy and ease.' But suddenly a sad mischance befell him because the final part of happiness is always misery. God alone knows that worldly joy is gone! If an author could competently describe it, he might confidently write about it in a chronicle as a thing supremely worthy of note.

Now every wys man lat him herkne me;
This storie is al so trewe, I undertake,
As is the book of Launcelot de Lake, — is that true?   445
That wommen holde in ful greet reverence.
Now wol I torne agayn to my sentence.
   A colfox ful of sly iniquitee,
That in the grove hadde wonned yeres three,   450
By heigh ymaginacioun forn-cast,
The same nyght thurgh-out the hegges brast
Into the yerd, ther Chauntecleer the faire
Was wont, and eek his wyves, to repaire;
And in a bed of wortes stille he lay   455
Til it was passed undren of the day,
Waitynge his tyme on Chauntecleer to falle;
As gladly doon thise homycides alle
That in await liggen to mordre men.

O false mordrour lurkynge in thy den,   460
O newe Scariot, newe Genyloun,
False dissymulour, O Greek Synoun,
That broghtest Troye al outrely to sorwe!
O Chauntecleer, acursed be that morwe
That thou into that yerd flaugh fro the bemes.   465
Thou were ful wel y-warned by thy dremes
That thilke day was perilous to thee;
But what that God forwoot moot nedes bee,
After the opinioun of certein clerkis.

Witnesse on hym that any parfit clerk is,   470
That in scole is greet altercacioun
In this mateere and greet disputisoun,
And hath been of an hundred thousand men;
But I ne kan nat bulte it to the bren
As kan the hooly doctour Augustyn,   475
Or Boece, or the bisshope Bradwardyn,
Wheither that Goddes worthy forwityng
Streyneth me nedely to doon a thyng —
Nedely clepe I symple necessitee;

Now I want every wise man to listen to me, as I guarantee that this episode is as true as the book of Lancelot du Lac, the person whom women hold in the greatest respect. Now, then, I shall return to what I was saying.

A fox, with black markings, which had dwelt three years in the grove, guided by wicked cunning, suddenly appeared, as had been foretold in Chantecleer's dream, that same night through the hedges into the yard where the fine Chantecleer was accustomed to resort with his wives. He lay quietly in a bed of vegetables till the forenoon had passed, waiting for his opportunity to fall upon Chantecleer in the same self-satisfied way that all these murderers, who lie in wait to murder people, do.

O false murderer lurking in his hideout! O modern Judas Iscariot! Modern Ganelon! False dissembler, Greek Sinon who brought Troy utterly to ruin! O Chantecleer, cursed is that morning that made you fly from the perches into the yard! Your dreams provided you with fair warning that this same day was dangerous for you. But, according to the opinion of certain scholars, what God knows beforehand must take place.

You may get proof from any excellent scholar that there is a hot dispute about this point among the scholars, an intense argument carried on by a hundred thousand men. I cannot, however, sift the flour from the bran in the same way as the pious doctor Augustine or Boethius or Bishop Thomas Bradwardine regarding the point whether God's noble foreknowledge forces us necessarily to perform an action (by 'necessarily' I mean 'simple necessity');

Or elles if free choys be graunted me 480
To do that same thyng or do it noght,
Though God forwoot it er that it was wroght;
Or if his wityng streyneth never a deel
But by necessitee condicioneel.
I wil nat han to do of swich mateere, 485
My tale is of a cok, as ye may heere,
That took his conseil of his wyf with sorwe,
To walken in the yerd upon that morwe
That he hadde met that dreem that I yow tolde.
Wommennes conseils been ful ofte colde; 490
Wommannes conseil broghte us first to wo
And made Adam fro Paradys to go,
Ther-as he was ful myrie and well at ese;

But for I noot to whom it myght displese,
If I conseil of wommen wolde blame, 495
Passe over, for I seyde it in my game.
Rede auctours, where they trete of swich mateere,
And what they seyn of wommen ye may heere;
Thise been the cokkes wordes and nat myne,
I kan noon harm of no womman divyne. 500
   Faire in the sond to bathe hire myrily
Lith Pertelote, and alle hire sustres by,
Agayn the sonne, and Chauntecleer so free
Song murier than the mermayde in the see.

For *Phisiologus* seith sikerly, 505
How that they syngen wel and myrily.
And so bifel that, as he cast his ye
Among the wortes on a boterflye,
He was war of this fox that lay ful lowe;
No-thyng ne liste hym thanne for to crowe, 510
But cride anon, 'Cok, cok,' and up he sterte,
As man that was affrayed in his herte.
For naturelly a beest desireth flee
Fro his contrárie, if he may it see,
Though he never erst hadde seyn it with his eye. 515

Or whether I possess free will either to do or not to do that very action, although God foresaw it before the action was done; or whether his foreknowledge only compels me by 'conditional necessity'. I am not going to interfere in this argument, for, as you can hear, my story merely concerns a cock, which sorrowfully sought the advice of his wife as to whether he should walk around the yard on the day after he had had the dream I have already described. 'Woman's counsel is often cold counsel.' It was woman's counsel that first brought us to unhappiness and compelled Adam to depart from Paradise where he was exceedingly happy and comfortable.

But I must be careful as to whom I might displease if I put blame on the counsel of women; I think you had better forget that as I merely said it for fun. You can read authors who discuss this matter and there you can learn what they say about women. These were the words of the cock, not mine. I know nothing to the disadvantage of women.

Pertelote was around, playing and bathing very happily in the sand, with all her sisters near her in the sun, while Chantecleer, feeling so gay, sang more happily than a mermaid in the sea.

Indeed, the 'Physiologus' describes very aptly how well and cheerily birds can sing. It so happened that, as he was looking among the vegetables for a butterfly, he became aware of the fox lying low there. He had no desire to crow at that moment. Instead, he cried out in terror and jumped up like a man completely scared in his heart, for naturally an animal, when he is aware of an enemy, wants to fly from it, though he may not have set eyes on the enemy before.

This Chauntecleer, whan he gan hym espye,
He wolde han fled, but that the fox anon
Seyde, 'Gentil sire, allas! wher wol ye gon?
Be ye affrayed of me that am youre freend?
Now certes I were worse than a feend,   520
If I to yow wolde harm or vileynye.
I am nat come your conseil for t'espye;
But trewely the cause of my comynge
Was oonly for to herkne how that ye synge;
For trewely ye have as myrie a stevene   525
As any aungel hath that is in hevene.
Therwith ye han in musyk moore feelynge
Than hadde Boece, or any that kan synge.

My lord youre fader (God his soule blesse!)
And eek youre mooder, of hire gentillesse,   530
Han in myn hous y-been to my greet ese,
And certes, sire, ful fayn wolde I yow plese.
But for men speke of syngyng, I wol seye,
So moote I brouke wel myne eyen tweye,
Save yow I herde never man so synge   535
As dide youre fader in the morwenynge.
Certes it was of herte, al that he song;
And for to make his voys the moore strong
He wolde so peyne hym that with bothe his eyen
He moste wynke, so loude he wolde cryen;   540

And stonden on his tiptoon therwithal,
And strecche forth his nekke, long and smal;
And eek he was of swich discrecioun
That ther nas no man in no regioun
That hym in song or wisedom myghte passe.   545
I have wel rad in Daun Burnel the Asse,
Among his vers, how that ther was a cok,
For that a preestes sone yaf hym a knok
Upon his leg, whil he was yong and nyce,
He made hym for to lese his benefice;   550

When Chantecleer noticed him, he wanted to fly away but the fox immediately spoke to him, 'Alas, noble sir, where do you wish to go? Are you frightened of me, your friend? Indeed, if I intended any ill or harm towards you, I should be worse than a devil. I have not come to spy into your secrets. The true reason for my coming was only to hear you sing. I must confess you possess as delightful a voice as any angel in heaven. Moreover, you put more feeling into your music than Boethius or anyone else who knows how to sing ever did.

My lord, your father – God bless his soul! – and also your mother in her kindness have visited my house and given me intense pleasure. But, as we have mentioned singing, I must say this – as sure as I hope to enjoy the use of my two eyes! – that, with the exception of yourself, I have never heard anyone sing so well as your father did in the morning. Indeed, everything he sang came from the heart and, in order to strengthen his voice, he would make such efforts with both his eyes that he would even close them when he sang very loudly.

He would also stand on the top of his toes, stretching forward his long, thin neck. Again, he was possessed of such exceptional powers of judgment that no one could surpass him in singing or wisdom. I have read, among the poems of Lord Burnell the Ass, how a priest's son caused his father to lose his appointment by breaking with a knock the leg of a young and foolish cock.

But certeyn ther nys no comparisoun
Bitwixe the wisedom and discrecioun
Of your fader and of his subtiltee.
Now syngeth, sire, for seinte charitee;
Lat se konne ye youre fader countrefete.'   555
This Chauntecleer his wynges gan to bete,
As man that koude his traysoun nat espie.
So was he ravysshed with his flaterie.
    Allas! ye lordes, many a fals flatour
Is in your courtes and many a losengeour,   560
That plesen yow wel moore, by my feith,
Than he that soothfastnesse unto yow seith.
Redeth Ecclesiaste of flaterye;
Beth war, ye lordes, of hir trecherye.

    This Chauntecleer stood hye upon his toos   565
Strecchynge his nekke, and heeld his eyen cloos,
And gan to crowe loude for the nones,
And daun Russell, the fox, stirte up at ones,
And by the gargat hente Chauntecleer,
And on his bak toward the wode hym beer;   570
For yet ne was ther no man that hym sewed.
    O destinee that mayst nat been eschewed!
Alas that Chauntecleer fleigh fro the bemes!
Allas his wyf ne roghte nat of dremes!
And on a Friday fil al this meschaunce.   575

O Venus, that art goddesse of pleasaunce,
Syn that thy servant was this Chauntecleer,
And in thy servyce dide al his poweer
Moore for delit than world to multiplye,
Why woldestow suffre hym on thy day to dye?   580
O Gaufred, deere maister soverayn,
That, whan thy worthy kyng Richard was slayn
With shot, compleynedest his deeth so soore,
Why ne hadde I now thy sentence and thy loore
The Friday for to chide, as diden ye?   585
For on a Friday, soothly, slayn was he.

But, of course, there is no comparison between the wisdom and discretion of your father and the subtlety of Gundulf's cock. Now, for holy love, sing up, sir! Let us see if you can imitate your father.' Chantecleer was so overwhelmed with his flattery that he began to beat his wings just like any man who did not suspect treachery would.

Gentlemen, many a false flatterer is in your courts and many a deceiver who, on my word of honour, may please you more than the person who tells you the truth. Read in Ecclesiasticus about flattery – 'Never trust thine enemy.'

Chantecleer stood high upon his toes, stretching out his neck, his eyes closed, and began to crow as loudly as possible for the supreme test. Lord Russell, the fox, leapt up immediately and grabbed him by the throat. As there was no one near to pursue him, he carried him across his back towards the wood.

O Destiny which cannot be avoided! Have pity on that Chantecleer who flew from the beams! Have pity upon his wife who cared not about his dreams! Worst of all, this misfortune happened on a Friday.

O Venus, the goddess of delights, why, since Chantecleer was your servant and did his utmost in your service, and more for personal pleasure than to increase the population, why should you allow him to die on your day? O Geoffroi de Vinsauf, dear supreme master who lamented your noble King Richard's death so bitterly when he was slain! Why do I not possess your wisdom and learning to reproach that black Friday in the way you did? For it was on a Friday that he was slain.

Thanne wolde I shewe yŏw how that I koude pleyne
For Chauntecleres drede and for his peyne.
   Certes swich cry ne lamentacioun
Was never of ladyes maad whan Ylioun   590
Was wonne, and Pirrus with his streite swerd
Whan he hadde hent kyng Priam by the berd
And slayn hym (as seith us *Eneydos*),
As maden alle the hennes in the clos,
Whan they had seyn of Chauntecleer the sighte.   595
But sovereynly dame Pertelote shrighte,
Ful louder than dide Hasdrubales wyf,
Whan that hir housbonde hadde lost his lyf
And that the Romayns hadde brend Cartage –
She was so ful of torment and of rage,   600
That wilfully into the fyr she sterte
And brende hirselven with a stedefast herte.
O woful hennes, right so criden ye
As, whan that Nero brende the citee
Of Rome, cryden the senatoures wyves,   605
For that hir husbondes losten alle hir lyves;
Withouten gilt this Nero hath hem slayn.
Now wol I torne to my tale agayn.

   This sely wydwe and eek hir doghtres two
Herden thise hennes crie and maken wo,   610
And out at dores stirten they anon
And syen the fox toward the grove gon
And bar upon his bak the cok away,
And cryden, 'Out! 'Harrow!' and 'Weylaway!'
'Ha! ha! the fox!' and after hym they ran,   615
And eek with staves many another man;
Ran Colle, oure dogge, and Talbot and Gerland,
And Malkyn with a dystaf in hir hand;
Ran cow and calf, and eek the verray hogges,
So were they fered for berkynge of the dogges   620
And shoutyng of the men and wommen eek;
They ronne so hem thoughte hir herte breek;

Then would I show you how I too could lament over the misfortune and sorrow of Chantecleer.

Indeed, such weeping or lamentation was never made by the women when Troy was captured; and Pyrrhus, when, with drawn sword, he had seized Priam by the beard and killed him (so the 'Aeneid' tells us), was never so lamented as was Chantecleer by all the hens in the yard when they saw his misfortune. Lady Pertelote shrieked as loud as she could, far louder than Hasdrubal's wife did when her husband lost his life or the Carthaginian women did when the Romans burnt Carthage. She was so overwhelmed with trouble and rage that, of her own accord, she jumped into the fire and, with a stoic heart, burnt herself. O troubled hens, you cried like the wives of the senators, who had innocently lost their lives, cried when Nero burnt the City of Rome (Nero had slain them). Now, I shall return once more to my story.

The innocent widow and her two daughters heard these hens crying in fear and, running outside at once, caught a glimpse of the fox running towards the grove, bearing the cock away on his back. 'Help! Murder! The Fox!' they cried and ran after him, accompanied by a crowd of people with sticks, Collie our dog, Talbot, Gerland and Malkin with the distaff in her hand; the cows and calves and even the pigs scattered, extremely frightened by the barking of the dogs and the shouting of the men and women. They ran so hard that it seemed to them their hearts would break.

They yolleden as feendes doon in helle;
The dokes cryden as men wolde hem quelle;
The gees for feere flowen over the trees;   625
Out of the hyve cam the swarm of bees;
So hydous was the noys, *a! benedicitee!*
Certes he Jakke Straw and his meynee
Ne made never shoutes half so shrille,
Whan that they wolden any Flemyng kille,   630
As thilke day was maad upon the fox.
Of bras they broghten bemes, and of box,
Of horn, of boon in whiche they blewe and powped,
And therwithal they shriked and they howped;
It seemed as that hevene sholde falle.   635

Now, goode men, I pray yow herkneth alle;
Lo! how Fortune turneth sodeynly
The hope and pryde eek of hir enemy.
This cok, that lay upon the foxes bak,
In al his drede unto the fox he spak   640
And seyde, 'Sire, if that I were as ye,
Yet wolde I seyn, as wys God helpe me,
"Turneth agayn, ye proude cherles alle;
A verray pestilence upon yow falle.
Now am I come unto the wodes syde,   645
Maugree youre heed the cok shal heere abyde;
I wol hym ete in feith, and that anon"'

The fox answerde, 'In feith it shal be don';
And, as he spak that word, al sodeynly
This cok brak from his mouth delyverly,   650
And heighe upon a tree he fleigh anon.
And whan the fox saugh that he was y-gon,
'Allas!' quod he, 'O Chauntecleer, allas!
I have to yow,' quod he, 'y-doon trespas,
In-as-muche as I maked yow aferd,   655
Whan I yow hente and broght out of the yerd
But, sire, I dide it of no wikke entente;
Com doun, and I shal telle yow what I mente;
I shal seye sooth to yow, God help me so.'

They kept on yelling like devils do in hell; the ducks quacked as if someone intended to kill them; the frightened geese flew over the trees; and the swarm of bees emerged from the hive. Praise be, the noise was terrific. Jack Straw and his followers could not have shouted half so shrilly when they wanted to kill a Fleming, as those did that day against the fox. They brought out beams of brass and boxwood, of horn and bone on which they blew and hooted, shrieking and shouting so much that it seemed as if heaven would fall.

Now, gentlemen, I beg you to listen closely. Listen how Fortune suddenly overturned the hope and pride of their enemy! As the cock lay across the fox's back, in all his fear, he said to the fox, "Sir, if I were you, as sure as fate I would say, turn back, all of you proud peasants. I hope a violent plague will fall upon you! Now that I have reached the border of this wood, the cock will remain here whatever you can do. Furthermore, I shall eat him straightaway."

'By heavens,' replied the fox, 'I shall do that.' And, as he spoke, the cock suddenly broke clear of his mouth as nimbly as he could and flew at once to the top of a tree. When the fox saw he had gone, he said, 'Shame on you, Chantecleer! Shame on you! The only wrong I have done towards you was that I made you afraid, when I seized you and brought you from the yard. Really, I did it with no wicked intent. Come down and I shall tell you what I intended. I promise I shall tell you the truth.'

'Nay thanne,' quod he, 'I shrewe us bothe two;   660
And first I shrewe myself, bothe blood and bones,
If thou bigyle me any ofter than ones.
Thou shalt na moore thurgh thy flaterye
Do me to synge and wynke with myn ye,
For he that wynketh, whan he sholde see,   665
Al wilfully, God lat him never thee.'
'Nay,' quod the fox, 'but God yeve hym meschaunce,
That is so undiscreet of governaunce
That jangleth when he sholde holde his pees.'

Lo! swich it is for to be recchelees   670
And necligent, and truste on flaterye.
But ye that holden this tale a folye,
As of a fox, or of a cok and hen,
Taketh the moralite, goode men;
For Seint Paul seith that all that writen is   675
To oure doctrine it is ywrite ywis;
Taketh the fruyt and lat the chaf be stille.
Now, goode God, if that it be thy wille,
As seith my lord, so make us alle goode men,
And brynge us to his heighe blisse. Amen.   680

'Oh, no,' said Chantecleer, 'I curse the two of us but I should curse myself, both blood and bones, more than you, if you will trick me more than once. Your flattery will not catch me again in making me sing and close my eyes, for the person who closes his eyes quite deliberately when he ought to keep them open, should not hope for God's help.' 'No,' replied the fox, 'but may God bring ill-luck to him who displays such indiscreet behaviour as to chatter when he should keep quiet.'

That is the consequence of being thoughtless, careless and too trusting in flattery. Unless you consider this story about a fox and a cock and hen pointless, you should heed of its moral, gentlemen. Paul says, 'For whatsoever things were written aforetime were written for our learning.' Take the corn and leave the husks.

Now, great God, if that is your will, (so says our Lord), make us all good-living men and bring us to heavenly bliss.

The Epiloge of
The Nonne Preestes Tale

'Sir Nonnes Preest,' our hoste seyde anoon,
'Y-blessed be thy breche, and every stoon!',
This was a mery tale of Chauntecleer,
But, by my troothe, if thou were seculer,
Thou woldest been a trede-foul a-right.   685
For, if thou have corage as thou hast might,
Thee were need of hennes, as I wene,
Ya, mo than seven tymes seventene.
See, which braunes hath this gentil Preest,
So greet a nekke, and swich a large breest!   690
He loketh as a sperhauk with his yen;
Him nedeth not his colour for to dyen
With brasil, ne with greyn of Portingale.
Now sire, faire falle you for youre tale!'

And after that he, with ful mery chere,   695
Seide to another, as ye shullen here.

The Epilogue of
The Nun's Priest's Tale

'Sir Nun's Priest,' our Host said straightaway, 'blessed be your breeches and each testicle! This story of Chauntecleer was a pleasant one, but, by my word, if you were not in holy orders, you would be a fine treader of hens. For, if your virility is equal to your strength, you would have need of hens, in my opinion, yes, more than seven times seventeen. See, what muscles this noble priest has, what a thick neck and broad chest! His eye has the look of a sparrow-hawk. He has no call for a red dye made from brazil (wood), nor one made from Portuguese grain. Now, sir, good fortune be yours for telling such a tale!'

And after that, with a most cheerful expression, he spoke to someone else, as you shall hear.

Textual notes

1 **Hoo** The tale of the Monk which preceded that of the Nun's Priest was so unsuited to the circumstances, as it consisted of a recital of cases of men who had been prosperous and had fallen from their high estate, that the Knight stopped him after nearly 800 lines had been spoken. The interjection 'hoo!' was used to interrupt a tournament: it would be familiar to the Knight who had fought thrice in the lists, as the *Prologue* tells us.

2 **y-wis** This adverb became corrupted into 'iwis', which was held to mean 'I know'. Translated by 'certainly'.

4 **gesse** Should think.

6 **where as** Here, and in many other places, the word 'as' is best left untranslated; it has little or no meaning in Modern English.

men This word is frequently used with an active verb to form a passive. Here 'one' would be a good translation, with a singular verb.

9 **hath** This is the normal form of the third person singular of a present tense in the East Midland dialect which Chaucer spoke.

12 **it thynketh me** An impersonal construction, common in Middle English. Translated by 'it seems to me' and not by 'I think'.

14 **seinte Poules belle** Harry Bailly, the host of the Tabard in Southwark, would doubtless be familiar with the sound of the Cathedral bell.

15 **clappeth** An appropriate word, suggesting that the tongue of the Monk was no more musical than that of the bell.

16 This line and the next include phrases from the Monk's last few words which somehow the Host had caught in spite of his drowsiness.

17 **noot** The word is contracted from *ne-woot*, meaning 'know not'. The initial *ne-* is found elsewhere merging with the beginning of the following verb and so making it negative.

19 **compleyne** A transitive verb, with a direct object.

22 **Sire** The usual title for a monk. It is used, in line 44, of the Priest.

26 **daun** Represents the Latin *dominus*, master.

24 **boterflye** The word seems a strange one to use. Dare we suggest that it was introduced as a sort of rhyme for 'compaignye'?

25 **desport** The Host had laid down that the Tales told on the pilgrimage should be entertaining and amusing. The Monk had transgressed this ruling.

28 nere See note to line 17. The verb is in the subjunctive here 'Were it not. . .'

clynkyng In his description of the Monk, Chaucer remarked on the bells on the bridle of the Monk's horse, and on the Monk's passion for hunting.

30 hevene Certain feminine nouns in Old English had no 's, or *es*, to mark the possessive case. Here we have an example in the word *hevene*, to be translated *heaven's*.

34 thise Used like Latin *ille* to suggest distinction, or importance.

42 rude speche The cultivated voices of the Knight and the Monk contrast with the rougher tones of the innkeeper.

44 neer This is a comparative word, meaning 'nearer'. The positive is 'ny'.

thou preest The words are intended to show politeness, no doubt, but the second person singular usually showed contempt, part possibly of the 'rude speche' of Harry Bailly.

50 so moot I go Go meant 'walk'. The expression means 'as ever I hope to enjoy the use of my legs'. It may be rendered by 'I can assure you', a much less vivid asserveration. Similar phrases are found elsewhere.

54 The Priest has not been described in the *General Prologue*. Here he is shown to be a companionable fellow, not like the Monk in his present mood.

55–80 These twenty-five lines give us the setting of the story: we are introduced to the widow who owned the cock and to her household.

58 which 'Who', 'whose', and 'whom' were interrogative pronouns in Chaucer's day, and not relative.

59 that . . . wyf That is, 'since her husband died'.

61 catel Property, not cattle.

rente Income.

62 housbondrie Economical use.

as God hire sente These words remind us that the speaker is a priest.

63 fond Supported. The word is still found in certain dialects with this meaning.

65 Malle Molly. The dogs of the village are also named, and of course the cock, the hen, and the fox.

66 sooty There were no chimneys in humble cottages.

bour Bedroom.

halle Living room. These words would be more appropriately applied to a lord's castle, a whimsical touch, of which we shall have many other examples.

68 hir neded An impersonal construction – 'there was necessary for her'.

deel 'drop, bit'.

70 cote Cottage. Her frugal diet was in keeping with her humble home.

72 Her rules for health were moderate diet, exercise, and a contented mind.

76 White wine came from Alsace, and red from Bordeaux.

77 'White and black' was found on her table White milk and black, or dark, bread. Remember that colours were not so precisely defined as they are now.

79 Seynd Broiled or grilled.

ey This southern English word for 'egg' has been driven out by the northern form of the word.

80 maner Kind of.

deye Dairywoman.

81 We are about to be introduced to the hero of the story. Notice how the Priest adds detail to detail, thus accumulating a mass of evidence for the fitness of the cock for his distinguished role. The villain is not mentioned yet: Chauntecleer occupies the whole stage, with his hens as his protégés, and certainly his inferiors.

84 In al the land of crowyng nas his peer The words mean, 'in all the land there was not his equal in crowing'; his name means 'the clear singer'.

85 murier Pleasanter, sweeter-sounding. The word meant something other than its modern meaning.

86 gon The word is plural, agreeing with the idea that an organ consists of a multiplicity of components. Orgon is singular.

87 sikerer More to be relied on. The superiority of the cock to a piece of mere mechanism is to be noted.

88 clokke The word is derived from the root suggesting a bell, and has a definite reference to a sound. A clokke would be driven by a spring, or weights, or even by water, and controlled by a pendulum, or a balance, like a modern clock. An orlogge would most likely refer to a sundial, a silent instrument for indicating time.

89 nature Instinct. Knowledge acquired laboriously by astronomers was instinctive to the cock.

90–1 The equinoctial is an imaginary circle, as it were an equator of the heavens. Another circle, representing the annual path of the sun through the heavens, cuts the former in two places, called the equinoxes where the days and nights are of equal lengths. The equinoctial circle was supposed to move round completely once in the twenty-four hours, that is, it moved through fifteen degrees every hour. It was at these intervals throughout the day that Chauntecleer crew, in other words at every hour.

90 **thilke toun** As the correct statement of the time depended upon the longitude in which the observer stood, the cock's timing was correct only for the village where he lived. Hence: 'in thilke toun'. 'Toun' is to be translated 'village', rather than 'town'.

91 As 'fifteen degrees' represents one-twenty-fourth of the circle, the cock evidently crowed once an hour.

92 **Might not be improved upon** A further testimony to his all-round superiority.

92 **batailled** Battlemented, a reference to the serrated comb of the bird.

96 **toon** plurals in -*n* were frequent in Old English, and were still to be found in Chaucer's day. Shakespeare uses 'shoon' for 'shoes'.

97 **flour** This spelling served for 'flower' till about 1740.

99 **gentil** Noble, well-born. A reference to his parents occurs in lines 530–55.

100 **Sevene** The perfect number, as would befit a super-cock.

103 'The one with the fairest colours on her throat.'

104 **damoysele** Mistress, a suitable word for the favourite wife. She is now described, but not in such detail, as Chauntecleer.

105 Courtly, tactful and gracious, and a good companion.

108 **hoold** Safe-keeping.

109 Fast bound to her in every limb, by his love for her.

110 **wel** A noun, 'happiness', 'a sense of well-being'.

hym 'To him', or 'his'.

113 **accord** Harmony. The words of the duet sung by Chauntecleer and Pertelote are no doubt those discovered by the noted Chaucerian scholar, Professor W. W. Skeat, in a manuscript in Trinity College, Cambridge. It was probably a well-known song of the period; Chaucer's hearers would no doubt know it and be amused at this reference to it.

in londe Far away.

115 The whole of the story depends on this assumption. The fox tells us about his own appreciation of music in lines 525–45.

120 **gan gronen** Groaned. 'Gan to gronen' would mean 'began to groan'.

121 **man** One.

122 **roore** A strange accomplishment for a cock. Translate, perhaps, by 'cry out'.

125 **verray** 'Fine', spoken in irony. The heroic cock has another side to his character; he is not a complete paragon.

127 **take it nat agrief** Don't make a grievance of my distress. He was rather hurt at her irony, for to him it was a real trouble.

128 **mette** Here, as often, the verb is used reflexively, with a dative. 'It came to me in my dream that I was . . .' Elsewhere, as in line 160, the verb is used with a personal subject: 'ye han met . . .'

130 **recche** Expound. The dream seems to suggest impending disaster; may God be able to find a happier interpretation.

132 **romed** 'Stalked', 'strutted'. A cock's legs would hardly be capable of 'roaming'.

134 Wanted to seize and kill me. 'Wolde' has more of the notion of purpose or intention than the modern 'would'.

136 Pertelote, a skilled amateur psychiatrist, finds clues to the trouble as her husband relates his dream in all its details. The 'operative' words are yelow, reed, and blak. Chauntecleer, nervous as any man might well be who believed dreams foretold what would certainly happen, must be reassured. His wife puts it down mostly to indigestion, a common-sense explanation, which however the cock cannot accept, as we hear later.

140 **Yet** Still. 'Even now I'm almost dead for fear of what he looked like.'

142 **Avoy!** 'Get away with you!' This is the implication of the exclamation.

132 **that** The great. The words of Pertelote are admirable; she speaks as a loving wife might well speak to reassure a husband who has temporarily lost his nerve. It will be noticed too that during the course of her remarks she loses the attributes of a hen and assumes those of a woman. Such references as 'fear of weapons', 'no man's heart', 'a beard', do not come from a hen on a perch, but rather from a lady in a castle, chiding her warrior husband. She has indeed called herself a 'woman' in line 146.

150 **agast** This was the usual spelling of the word until the early printers, who had been taught their craft in Holland, spelt the word with the extra 'h', as was the Dutch custom.

154 The cock is now a bearded warrior, terror-stricken.

155 **konne ye** 'Is it possible that you are . . .?'

159 The doctors of the time were taught that bodily health depended upon the equilibrium of four factors, called 'humours'. These were fluids, known as melancholy, phlegm, blood and bile, of which the last three certainly exit. When these were mixed in the right proportions the patient was well; but when any irregularity occurred, the bodily health was thrown out of gear, and illness resulted. Moreover, the

humours were characterized as possessing the usual qualities of matter: melancholy was cold and dry; phlegm, cold and moist; blood, hot and moist; and bile, hot and dry. The combining of the humours was called 'complexion', and controlled a person's temperament. The treatment of a malady consisted of bleeding, if the blood were in excess, and of purging, if the fault was in the other humours.

160 **to-nyght** We should say: 'last night', keeping 'to-night' for the night not yet passed. The matter-of-fact wife reminds her husband of the principal causes of dreams, and so tries to relieve him of his fears; everyone has these experiences.

162 The excess of 'red' bile causes the dreamer to see red things in his dreams: arrows, with blood on the tips, fire, red-coated animals, bloody fighting, and dogs attacking one another.

167 The excess of 'black' bile accounts for the presence of black bears and bulls, and black devils. The animal like a dog had black ears and a black tip to its tail. Its appearance in the dream is thus explained. There was no need for the lady to tell of other excesses producing other effects: she has done all that was really necessary. She fortifies her diagnosis by a line from a Latin author her husband might have read at school.

174 **Catoun** This is not the Cato who so persistently demanded the destruction of Carthage in the second century B C, but an obscure writer of whom almost nothing is known, except that his couplets were used in schools in Chaucer's time. We may be surprised that the lady knew of this Latin text, but it had been translated into English.

177 **as taak** Be sure to take, the 'as' introducing a gentle, tactful recommendation.

185 **tho** These, not those.

186 'Which have by their very nature the property of purging you. . .'

189 **coleryk of compleccioun** Overcharged with bile, momentarily.

190 **ascencioun** Rising towards midday, its moment of greatest power.

191 **humours hoote** Choler and blood both produced heat.

195 **Here is the prescription** Worms to cure the digestive upset, to be followed by purgative herbs after two days or so. The herbs mentioned are listed in one or other of the herbals compiled about this time, or shortly afterwards. It is fortunate that the widow had them all in her garden, she would not have needed them herself: perhaps her daughters were not so careful of their diet as their mother was.

197 **lawriol** Usually identified with spurge laurel, a powerful purgative.

centaure 'For inward diseases; 'tis very wholesome, but not very toothsome'.

fumetere Fumitory, 'for clarifying the blood from saltish, choleric humours'.

ellebor Stinking hellebore, 'very effectual against all melancholic diseases'.

katapuce The lesser spurge.

gaitrys beryis Buckthorn berries, 'very effectual against the jaundice'.

herbe-yve Possibly a plantain, which 'helpeth weak stomachs which cannot retain their meat' – the world has nothing to do with 'ivy'. (The quotations in this note are from Culpeper's *Herbal*, of 1653.)

200 **that mery is** Where it is so pleasant.

202 Reference to the ancestors of the cock are made later by the fox. Lines 530–55.

204 Chauntecleer is not convinced. The talk took place during the night, a difficult time in which to cheer up a despondent person. He answers Pertelote's sensible suggestions by references to several authorities whose works he has studied.

205 The reference by Pertelote to Cato produced the avalanche of anecdotes and comments which occupies lines 218 to 384, or roughly one-quarter of the whole poem. Structurally the line 175 is of the greatest importance, for without it Chauntecleer would hardly have supplied all this evidence to disprove Cato's advice.

205–17 He refutes the testimony of Cato. Learned this age may be, but greater authorities do not support his advice: they teach that dreams *do* point to what is coming, whether good or bad.

207 **to drede** This phrase is used as both active and passive; here it is passive.

209 **Of many a man** Written by many a man.

210 **so moot I thee** Literally, 'so may I prosper'. It is a mild oath, meaning 'if what I say is not true, then may I not prosper'.

thee A verb.

214 Dreams may point, perhaps, to good fortune. See his remark in line 130.

216 Argument is a formal proof, set out step after step in logical order. There is no need for this, the anecdotes speak for themselves.

217 The real test is seen in the actual happening.

218 Chauntecleer launches into a recital of several anecdotes, derived from many sources, showing the importance of attending to the warnings offered in dreams. Disasters are recorded for neglect, rather than rewards for heeding the advice offered.

Oon of the gretteste auctours The reference is probably to Cicero, who tells the incident in his *De Divinatione*. He actually tells the second tale, see lines 301–38, before this one. Possibly Chaucer refers to Valerius

Maximus, who though less esteemed nowadays was far more popular in the Middle Ages than Cicero. He also tells both stories and in Cicero's order.

men rede We read.

219 **felawes** Friends, not 'fellows' in the loose sense in which the word is used today. The priest might almost have added: 'Just as we are doing now'.

222 Chaucer changes his construction here. 'Such a crowd of people' should be followed by such a phrase as 'and such a lack of accommodation'.

224 **o** One. Emphatic.

228 **hostelrye** Used ironically, perhaps. Each went to an inn; one had a comfortable room, while the other slept in a cowshed.

228–9 **gooth and took** Nowadays such a failure to observe sequence of tenses would not be tolerated; but see note to line 268.

231 **Fer in a yeerd** The idea of remoteness is well suggested: a cowshed, and that away from human help.

236 **This man** That is the one last mentioned.

237 **gan ... calle** See note on line 120.

244 **turned hym** Turned on to the other side.

245 **nas but** Was nothing but an illusion.

247 **yet** Once more.

252 **shaltow** Shalt thou (cf. maistow, line 340).

254 **do ... arresten** *Faire arrêter*, in modern French, 'have the cart stopped'.

256 **point** Detail. Chauntecleer emphasizes this detail as he had the details of his own dream.

266 **fallen in suspecioun** The reference is to the friend of the victim, who became suspicious.

268 **gooth** The present tense suggests vividness.

lette 'Delay'; as frequently in Shakespeare's English also.

270 **as it were** As though it were going on its usual errand.

273 **crye** Cry for, demand.

275 **this same nyght** See note on line 160, 'this very night'.

276 This detail was not revealed in the dream, as reported above.

lith gapyng upright Lies on his back with his mouth agape.

278 **sholden kepe** Ought to watch over.

279 **Harrow!** Alas, help! – a cry of distress, repeated in line 614.

heere In this cart.

283 **al newe** Quite recently.

284–9 These words might very well be the comment of the priest who is telling the story.

285 **biwreyest** Revealest. Not to be translated by 'betrayest'. The word is found in the Authorized Version of the Bible, Matthew, 26,73.

286 **Mordre wol out** This seems to be the first record of this belief.

287 **abhomynable** The 'h' is included from the mistaken idea that the word is connected with Latin 'homo', and that it means 'away from what a man would do'. Really it belongs to the root 'omen' and suggests the idea of a curse: 'ab-omin-able'.

288 **resonable** Fair, equitable; not 'reasonable' in its modern sense.

298 Chauntecleer is not satisfied by relating one instance; he provides another from the same Latin author.

300 **gabbe** Talk idly. He can give chapter and verse.

so have I joye or bliss; cf. line 210. 'If this is not true, may I forfeit my happiness in the next world.'

301–5 There is no main verb in this passage.

302 **certeyn** Definite. In our modern use, the word 'certain' means 'unspecified'.

306 **agayn** Towards, as in line 312. 'Against' is sometimes heard in dialect with a similar meaning.

310 **herkneth** This word is found in some manuscripts after 'but'. The line is then two syllables too long. It may be that the priest detects some lack of attention to his story, and is thus rebuking the offenders, or that he habitually in his preaching uses the word to the congregation in church. The story he is telling should hold the attention of the pilgrims.

318 **viage** The word does not necessarily refer to a sea journey, though it does so here.

319 **As for** As far as that day is concerned.

321 **full faste** Volubly, as from a well-stocked vocabulary.

323 **lette** Hinder, delay. There were in Old English two verbs, *lettan* and *lætan*, the former meaning 'to hinder' and the latter 'to permit'. These two became so confused in Middle English that one could not be distinguished from the other. In Modern English the word no longer has the meaning of 'to hinder' but retains that of 'to permit'. The word 'to let' in the sense of 'to grant temporary possession of' derives from the 'permit' verb: the term used in certain sports – a *let* ball – belongs to the 'hinder' idea.

thynges Business, the things I intend to do.

324 **sette not a straw by** Care not a fig for.

326 **al day** Continually, not continuously.

330 **forslewthen wilfully thy tyde** Deliberately lose your time through sloth. 'Tyde' means 'time' not 'tide', as also in line 338.

331 **it reweth me** I deeply regret it, an impersonal use, 'and goodbye to you'.

333 **cours** The distance planned.

339 The mention of Pertelote reminds us that Chauntecleer was retailing the anecdotes to his wife to convince her of the importance of dream-warnings.

344 **Seint Kenelm** He succeeded his father Kenulph as King of Mercia at the age of seven. The boy's sister, Cwenthryth, is said to have ordered his murder, of which he was warned in a dream. In the church at Winchcombe, Gloucestershire, can be seen two stone coffins recently found which are held to be those of Kenelm and his father, who visited the town frequently as he moved from place to place. The Abbey of Hailes, a few miles from Winchcombe, was dedicated to him, according to legend; but the very existence of the boy-king is doubtful.

351 **For** Against, because of.

354 **my sherte** My shirt of mail. The cock has become a baron again; see line 154. This alternation between Chauntecleer as bird and as man is a notable feature of the humour of the poem.

355 A legend of the saint would be read in church on the saint's day. The Pardoner is said in the *Prologue* of the Tales to be especially skilled at reading the story.

357 Macrobeus, who lived about the year AD 400, wrote a commentary on the *Somnium Scipionis* of Cicero. Scipio is said to have had a dream in which his grandfather foretold that he would conquer the Carthaginians. Most of the dreams recalled by Chauntecleer predicted some disaster; this is one of the few which did not. See line 214.

362 **of** About. The old Testament story of Daniel records several interpretations of dreams by him, and their fulfilment.

365 **sometyme** Chauntecleer seems to give away part of his case; how can it be known which dreams are not to be considered as warnings?

367 **daun Pharao** The dreams of Pharaoh of Egypt and of his butler and baker were interpreted by Joseph. See Chapters 40 and 41 of Genesis.

370 **seken** Search.

actes annals, records.

remes Kingdoms. Chauntecleer goes on to mention some details of what the records contain. The 'history' is legend rather than fact. The last of the examples of the downfall of kings, related by the monk before the knight stopped him, was that of Croesus of Lydia.

375 **heere** Listen to, attend to.

376 **sholde** Was fated to.

377 **same nyght biforn** The very night before.

384 Chaucer lets the cock's list of examples come to an end before it becomes as wearisome as the monk's recital had done. Notice the excellent reason for the cessation of the tales: the dawn was breaking, and Chauntecleer had work to do. He is not convinced by the suggestion of Pertelote that his digestion was out of order. The laxatives were poisonous, and he cannot trust them, the hero continues to be heroic.

392 **so have I blis** 'So may I have joy'.

393 **Of o thyng** In one respect.

394 The beauty of the face of his wife helps to add to the prestige of the hero.

395 **scarlet reed** A laying hen is characterized by this scarlet colour. The hero rejoices in his hen's prowess as a layer. See line 579.

397 **In principio** These are the first words, in the Vulgate, of the Gospel according to St John. The first fourteen verses were held to have almost magical powers. The two words here are equivalent to such a phrase as 'gospel truth'.

398 The Latin means, 'As surely as gospel truth, woman is man's ruin.' Chauntecleer turns the saying on its head and gives it an opposite meaning in his translation. It is possible that he is taking advantage of his wife's ignorance here but much more likely that he is displaying his own – his claims to knowledge are part of his vanity.

405 **sweven and dreem** There seems little distinction between the two words, although one might carry the overtone of 'vision'.

408 **chuk** In imitation of the noise of the bird.

409 As is so often the case, the relative is omitted in this line.

410 **Real** Regal, royal – as in 'Mont*real*', the royal mountain.

413 The hero now looks like the most kingly of animals.

414 Rometh must mean 'struts', as he is on tip-toe; his pride does not allow him to tread on the ground.

418 The hero is now a prince in his banqueting hall. He reaches the highest station he is destined to reach; his downfall is imminent.

419 **pasture** Feeding, meal, not pasture. He was in a farmyard.

420 A distinct break in the story is found here. The preliminaries are over, and the adventure is in preparation.

421 The Venerable Bede says that the world was created on March 18; the year is not stated. Lines 421 to 424 suggest that the date of the crisis in the life of Chauntecleer was May 2. March has thirty-one days; add to this number the thirty-two days of line 424; sixty-three days after March 1 brings us to May 3. The sun enters the sign of Taurus

on April 11; twenty-one days later is May 2. The 'som-what moore' of line 429 gives us May 3 also. We have been told before of Chauntecleer's amazing instinct, see line 89. Here is another example of his intuitive knowledge. This very complicated and confusing way of calculating the date may be no more than Chaucer's little joke at the expense of medieval astronomers and their methods of calculation.

431 **pryme** 9 a.m. It has been calculated – but Chauntecleer knew it without any calculation – that on May 3 the sun would actually have reached forty-one degrees in the latitude of the British Isles. Chaucer was interested in astrology and wrote a book on the subject for 'Little Lowis my Son', but much of it is either lost or was not completed.

434 She is no longer *hominis confusio*.

435–6 These lines have a very attractive lilt, especially if the final 'e' of each line is sounded. They seem to echo the cock's feeling of 'revel' and 'solas'.

438 'Pride goeth before destruction, and a haughty spirit before a fall.' No doubt the priest remembered this warning from the book of *Proverbs*. The transitory nature of happiness had been the theme of the monk's dismal tale: it was a common theme of medieval writers.

441 **rethor** Orator, or master of written eloquence.

endite Express his feelings in writing.

442 **cronycle** A record of fact.

443 **sovereyn notabilitee** Something supremely worthy of note.

444 The priest is about to enter upon an important section of the Tale, leading to the *dénouement*: he calls the hearers to pay special attention, as he had done once before at line 310.

446 As the book of Launcelot of the Lake is a romance, the priest must have said this with his tongue in his cheek: he despised the female intelligence.

447 **That** The relative pronoun may refer to either the book or the knight, and probably to the latter.

reverence Respect.

449 **colfox** A fox with much black in its coat, now usually called a brant-fox. Refer to lines 137 and 138 for the description of the fox seen in the cock's dream.

sly Cunning. His patience is also worth noting.

451 The line is not easy to understand, but from what follows in lines 468 to 485 we may suppose that there is a reference to God's foreknowledge of what was about to happen. On the other hand, the 'high imagination' may be that of the hero of the story; he had pictured this situation in his dream.

452 That very night, namely, the night of the dream.

452 **ther** Whither.

455 **stille** Quite.

456 **undren** The forenoon between 9 a.m. and noon.

457 **Waitynge** Watching his opportunity, biding his time.

459 **await** A noun meaning 'ambush'.

460 Sir John now apostrophizes three persons, two from romances, noted for their treachery.

461 **Scariot** Judas Iscariot, who betrayed Jesus Christ. Genyloun was the traitor in the Romance of Roland; he brought about the defeat of the army of Charlemagne at Roncevalles.

462 Synoun persuaded the Trojans treacherously to bring the wooden horse into the city, as related in the *Aeneid*.

463 **al outrely** Is a strong phrase – to the depths of despair.

468 Notice the juxtaposition of the two ideas, of the foreknowledge of God, and of the cock's prophetic dream. The placing of these side by side produces a humorous effect.

469 **clerkis** Scholars, one of whom, the Clerk of Oxford, was in the present company.

470 **Witnesse on hym** Call him as witness.

471 The University 'Schools'.

473 Multitudes of learned men have discussed the problems to be mentioned in the following lines, but the priest cannot satisfy himself of where the truth lies: he gives it up, and returns to the story.

475 **Augustyn** Bishop of Hippo and son of St Monica. He had, it would seem, settled the problem of God's foreknowledge and man's free will to his own satisfaction; but the discussion continued.

476 **Boece** He was Boethius, who wrote one of the great theological books of the early middle Ages – *De Consolatione Philosophiæ* – and is referred to again in line 528. His work had been translated into English by King Alfred and again by Chaucer himself. He died in 524.

Bradwardyn Archbishop of Canterbury, died of the Black Death in 1349. He believed implicitly in the foreknowledge of God, but there were possibilities for a man's choice, owing to God's own grace vouchsafed to him.

487 **with sorwe** With disastrous results.

490 **colde** Chilling, depressing, baneful. We should not blame the cock, the priest suggests, so many disasters have followed (women's) advice, notably the expulsion of Adam from Paradise.

494 **But for I noot** But because I do not know whom I might displease. The teller is in the group surrounding the prioress; he must avoid giving her offence, and Chaucer himself must not alienate the good offices of the ladies at the King's Court, to whom he no doubt read this *Tale*.

497 Most medieval writers would condemn the advice given by women.

499 **the cokkes wordes** Probably Chaucer was referring to lines 385–90.

500 **divyne** Guess, or impute to. Here he goes to the other extreme; he knows no woman whose suggestions might be harmful in any way.

501 After the digression, beginning at line 468, the priest takes up the story. We have a picture of a happy scene in the yard: the hen with her six attendants, and the cock singing – but not this time the duet of line 113. He has evidently forgotten his dream: joy has come with the morning.

505 Phisiologus is a book and not an author. It contained accounts of fabulous creatures and their accomplishments with warnings not to be beguiled by their blandishments. We recall the struggle of Ulysses to avoid the Sirens.

508 The butterfly may well have been a cabbage white!

510 **No-thyng** An adverb, meaning 'not at all, by no means'.

511 **Cok, cok** Evidently a cry of distress, different from the 'chuk' of line 407.

513 **The cock had never seen a fox** He did not know what animal it was who appeared in the dream: but instinct told him that he was face to face with his natural foe. Chauntecleer's instinct has been mentioned before.

516 **This** Our hero.

gan . . . espye Espied, noticed.

518 **Gentil sire** The opening words are a form of flattery.

wher Whither.

520 **I were** Subjunctive – 'I would be'.

521 **wolde** Intended.

vileynye Ill-treatment.

522 **conseil** Secrets, plans.

524 The fox's flattering is well brought out here. The cock had been singing when he spied the fox: the song gave Russell an opening.

528 Boethius, see line 476, had written a treatise on music, *De Musica*.

530 **hire gentillesse** Their kindness of heart, good feeling.

533 **for men speke** While we are speaking.

534 A mild oath; 'may I enjoy my two eyes': in other words, 'may I lose my sight if what I say is not true'.

538 A cunning suggestion. If Chauntecleer is to excel his father's performance he must make use of every device.

539 **peyne hym** Exert himself.

540 He must close both his eyes, stand on tiptoe, and stretch his neck. Then no one in the region could surpass the younger bird either.

546 There are, of course, foolish cocks, and some harbour malice; but Chauntecleer and his father were not of that temperament.

wel rad Read to my profit. Burnel the Asse, the little brown fellow, wanted a longer tail, but in his travels to find it, he lost half the short tail he had. Thereupon he decided to attend the University of Paris to become a scholar. He meets one, Arnold, who tells him the story of the cockerel here referred to. A priest's son had injured the leg of a young bird, who bided his time for revenge. The opportunity came when the young man, many years afterwards, wished to be roused early one morning so as to present himself before the Bishop for ordination. The cock deliberately refrained from crowing that morning; the man overslept, and failed to present himself in time. He was not consecrated and became a beggar.

549 **nyce** Foolish.

552 **wisedom and discrecioun** See lines 543 and 545.

553 **his** The cockerel's.

subtiltee Cunning.

554 **Seinte charitee** Holy charity.

559–64 These lines can hardly have been addressed by the priest to the pilgrims: they must be Chaucer's comment to his listeners when he was reading his poems, possibly before Richard II.

563 **Ecclesiaste** The reference is to a passage in the apocryphal book of Ecclesiasticus, 12, 10–16.

567 **for the nones** This phrase, which means 'for the occasion', is often used by the poet to fill out a line with very little meaning. But here the meaning is important: this was a great occasion in the experience of Chauntecleer. It will be noticed that the fox's suggestions and reminiscences of the father's deportment have all been adopted.

568 Russell, the little red fellow (cf. Burnel, the little brown fellow, line 546).

571 **sewed** Give chase. Now follows an interval during which we may suppose the theft has been discovered and some kind of chase organized.

572 **that mayst nat been eschewed** A reference to the predestination controversy which the priest had passed by, lines 468–85.

574 **roghte** Past tense of 'rekke', to heed.

575 The reference to Friday gives Chaucer another hare to pursue. Friday is an unlucky day.

576 **Venus** Friday, in Latin *dies veneris*, is the day of Venus, the goddess of pleasure, and she had forsaken her devotee, Chauntecleer. He and

Pertelote had great happiness in being together. The eggs they produced, we read, were a sure sign of their love for one another.

580 This line would seem to be misleading: we shall find that he did not die on her day. It intensifies our interest, however, in the fate of the splendid, though foolish, cock.

581 **Gaufred** Geoffrey de Vinsauf was connected with the University of Paris, and had set down rules which poets should follow to produce the elegant verses which the schoolmen required. Chaucer learned much from him but in time completely surpassed him. Geoffrey was an Englishman, who wrote an elegy on the death of Richard I as an example of elegiac verse. Chaucer, possibly ironically, calls for his help on the great occasion of what seemed likely to be the deplorable death of Chauntecleer, the king of fowls, as it were.

583 **shot** That is, an arrow. He was wounded on a Friday, but lingered some days before he died.

587 **yow** Chaucer has not been strictly careful over his second personal pronouns. In 582 he uses thy; a singular verb in 583; two singulars in 584; but ye, plural, in 585, and yow in 587. All these pronouns and adjectives seem to refer to Vinsauf. Possibly yow refers to the audience, however.

590 **Ylioun** Ilium, the citadel of Troy. After the treachery of Sinon, see line 462, the gates of Troy were opened to the Greeks and the Trojan king, Priam, slain by the Greek Pyrrhus, son of Achilles.

591 **streite swerd** In Latin *stricta ense*, with sword drawn.

593 **Eneydos** The word means not Aeneas, but the *Aeneid*.

596 **sovereynly . . . shrighte** Above them all . . . shrieked. The noise would be unusual for a hen to make; but Chauntecleer 'groaned' in line 120, and 'roared' in line 122.

600 **She** Refers to the wife of Hasdrubal.

601 **wilfully** Deliberately.

606 **losten alle** All lost.

Withouten gilt Who were guiltless.

607 He broke off the narrative at line 558. The pursuit of the fox has now been prepared: 'organized' would not be the right word to use.

609 We return to the widow of line 55, the first line of the *Tale*. All the events took place, up to this point, in her garden.

610 **maken wo** Show their distress.

612 **grove** The same as in line 57. It was the home of the fox. Gon and bar (613) are infinitives; 'go' and 'carry'.

614 'Come out; help; alas. Look out, the fox.'

616 Man is probably impersonal, and should be trannslated 'one'. See l. 621.

617 **oure dogge** It is not clear to whom the 'oure' refers. The three dogs are given names often given to dogs in the Middle Ages.

618 Malkyn is a name commonly given to an untidy domestic worker. But this one was evidently busy at her spinning. She figures with her distaff in many a grotesque carving under misericords in different parts of the country.

623 **doon** 'do', not 'down'.

627 **a! benedicitee!** God bless us all!

628 **he** That fellow Jack Straw. This is one of the very few references in the works of Chaucer to contemporary events. His revolt took place in 1381. He led an attack on London from Blackheath in order to secure redress of grievances: soon after his entrance into the city, a massacre of the Flemish wool-traders began. As Chaucer was living in London, at Aldgate, he doubtless heard something of the noise of the rioters.

632 **bemes** Here the word means 'trumpets': elsewhere in the *Tale* a word similarly spelt meant 'perches'.

614–35 A careful reading will show how many contributary noises swelled the din of the pursuers. The extra peril of bee-stings should not be overlooked.

636 The priest is nearing the point of the *Tale*. This is his third appeal for attention. As the pilgrims must have been stretched in a line along the highway, and each on his animal, he may have wanted to halt them for the conclusion, and the application to those present. He could hardly expect his voice to carry above the noise of the horses' hoofs on the highway. We may even wonder how it was that any of the riders heard the stories at all, or even whether they did get more than an occasional snatch or two.

642 **as wys God helpe me** As surely as God may help me; 'wys' is an adverb.

644 **A verray pestilence . . .** Plague take you all.

646 **Maugree youre heed** In spite of your head, in spite of any ruse you can think of.

649 **al sodeynly** Without the slightest warning.

654 I have wronged you deeply.

661 **bothe blood and bones** To the depths of my being.

664 **Do me to synge** Make me sing.

666 **thee** Prosper. Not to be mistaken for the pronoun.

665–6 This is the lesson the cock draws from the unpleasant incident.

667–9 The fox takes this lesson to himself.

670–1 The Nun's Priest suggests this moral to the company.

673 **As of** Because it concerns a cock and a fox, and not human beings.

674 **Take the lesson to heart** The *Tale* is told for your instruction.

678 The priest calls for God's blessing on the audience, as though he had been preaching in church.

679 Perhaps the benediction was that used by William Courteney, Archbishop of Canterbury from 1381–1396.

680 **heighe blisse** Happiness on high.

681 The Host is characteristically outspoken, even coarse in his appreciation of the Nun's Priest and his *Tale*. He comments on his manly appearance and speculates on what the Priest's sexual appetites would be were he 'seculer' (i.e. a layman). It may seem incongruous that such a light and balanced story comes from such a physically imposing individual.

Chaucer's narrative art in *The Nun's Priest's Tale*

A brief summary of the action of the poem (see *Plot*) suggests how little really happens in *The Nun's Priest's Tale*. The story might be told in a few lines, like some of Aesop's fables, but Chaucer chooses to extend it to more than 600. The elaboration and ornamentation of the tale far outweigh in length the substance of the story itself. The narrative is, again and again, interrupted by the story-teller's moralizing or instructive asides, by complicated comparisons, by stories-within-stories.

These digressions are inserted into the poem partly for their own sake and intrinsic interest. They also tell us something about the characters; for example, the dream narratives (lines 218–384) give Chauntecleer the chance to show off the range and variety of his knowledge, as does the list of cases from the Bible and classical sources where dreams have provided a truthful picture of some (usually disastrous) future. That he takes his own dreams so seriously reinforces his – and our – notion of his dignity, an important aspect of his character. Similarly, the Nun's Priest's digression on the subject of predestination (470–84) is obviously in keeping with his religious calling.

It should also be noted that some of these additions to the simple narrative appear curiously and ironically self-defeating. The long passage on dreams referred to above is delivered by Chauntecleer with force and earnestness, yet within moments the cock has forgotten the lesson he has himself been teaching because, as he says to Pertelote, 'whan I se the beautee of youre face ... It maketh al my drede for to dyen.' His words are wasted, not least on himself. In similar fashion, the story-teller will raise a subject of no direct relevance to the central narrative only to drop it after a few lines: 'I will nat han to do of swich mateere' he says of the vexed subject of predestination, even though he is the one responsible for introducing the subject in the first place; 'Passe over, for I seyde it in my game,' he hurriedly and prudently adds when talking about the bad advice women might give (he must avoid offending the Prioress). At first glance, such digressions may appear to be doubly pointless. Not only do they distract us from the narrative, but any advice or information they contain can be easily discarded or ignored in the course of the story. The very superfluity of these additions to the tale becomes almost an end in itself, as ornamental and as useless as Chauntecleer's comb which is 'redder than the fyn coral'. In fact, as already indicated, the way in which Chauntecleer or the Nun's Priest deals with the digressions they themselves have introduced into the narrative tells us something about *them*. As well, the asides and excursions often have an instructive, moralistic or simply entertaining function.

From the viewpoint of the unfolding narrative, the frequent interruptions should serve to sharpen our appetite to know what will happen next. Take the last quarter of *The Nun's Priest's Tale* as evidence of Chaucer's skill in manipulating his audience. After the fox's successful flattery of the cock, the narrator slips in a warning about the dangers of flattery (559–64). When the fox has snatched Chauntecleer and is making towards the wood, we do not hear immediately of the uproar this causes in the farmyard or of the noisy pursuit which follows. Instead the story-teller fires several one-line exclamations at us ('O destinee that mayst nat been eschewed!' etc) concluding with the rather anti-climactic detail that all this took place on a Friday. The tenuous relevance of this is revealed in the following section: Friday is the day associated with Venus, the goddess of love, in whose service the cock had worked so manfully 'moore for delit than world to multiplye'. There is then a mock-serious appeal to Venus, 'Why woldestow suffre hym on thy day to dye?' Our return to the story is further delayed by references to the death of Richard I (1199), which occurred on a Friday, and an elegy written on that death by a poet with whom Chaucer, perhaps ironically, compares himself. When the Nun's Priest does get back to his story, his description of the effect of Chauntecleer's capture on the hens in the farmyard is so overlaid by classical comparisons (see the note on *Irony* for further discussion of this topic) that the original reason for the outcry is almost lost sight of – and only then, after this extended (and half absurd) set of comparisons, does the teller say, 'Now wol I torne to my tale agayn'. The rest of the story proceeds straightforwardly with a very lively description of the chase after the fox (609–35) and an account of how the cock outwits his enemy and wins his freedom (639–69), although even here the poet cannot resist interjecting into the narrative a fairly standard comment on Fortune in some lines (636–8) which act as a kind of buffer between the picture of the pursuers and that of the pursued.

It is apparent, therefore, that the unfolding of the tale is far from smooth. Even in the last part of the story, as the pace quickens, we are diverted from the main track of events several times. Chaucer, in the person of the Nun's Priest, knows how far to stretch our patience in his exploration of some minor side-path before bringing us back, occasionally with a slightly self-satisfied comment, to the central narrative.

The digressions and asides in the poem are an essential, integral part of the work. They could not be removed, so that a 'pure' story remained, because they are a reflection of and commentary upon that story and, ultimately, its teller. The digressions inform us about character, they remind us (particularly in the dream-narratives) of the wider world outside the little farm, they amuse and instruct, and above all they offer living proof of the story-teller's art, as the narrative rushes forward, meanders or, suspended at some vital moment, pauses for breath.

The characters

The principal character of *The Nun's Priest's Tale* is a bird, the cock Chauntecleer. All the other figures in the story are subsidiary to him and can be briefly described.

A *widow* owns the farm where Chauntecleer lives. She is poor, quite old, careful in her management of her small-holding, frugal in her taste and happy in her circumstances:

'Attempree deite was al hir phisik,
And exercise, and hertes suffisaunce.'

After some 25 lines of such description she is relegated to the background until the chase at the tale's climax. The extreme simplicity of the widow's way of life and her surroundings provides an ironic framework for the comparative splendour of the birds in her farmyard.

Pertelote, Chauntecleer's 'wife', is described in terms suitable for a court lady: she is 'curteys . . . discreet and debonaire . . . compaignable'. Her function in the story is to act as a foil to her husband. When he tells her how frightened he has been by a dream, she rebukes him for his cowardice and informs him that she, like all women, desires to have a husband who is 'hardy, wise and free' etc. Her advice, which is well-meant but proves wrong, is to ignore the dream because it springs from overeating or some bodily imbalance and her common-sense remedy is that Chauntecleer should 'taak som laxatyf'. She promises to instruct him in the purgative properties of the various herbs that grow in the farmyard. Her beauty – we are told that because of it 'trewely she hath the herte in hoold/Of Chauntecleer' – and her briskness in dealing with his nightmare combine to make the cock reject the dream warning. The fact that she is wrong in her advice allows the Nun's Priest to touch lightly on a conventional medieval sore point – 'Wommannes conseil broghte us first to wo/And made Adam fro Paradys to go'.

The fox, *Daun* (a title of respect, 'sir' or 'master') *Russell*, has the characteristics associated with that animal in folklore. He is glib and persuasive, sly and unscrupulous. The story-teller likens him to famous murderers or traitors of the past and uses him as a means of warning 'ye lordes' against flattery.

Chauntecleer is the most fully realized character. He is proud and expansive in his appearance and appetites, unlike his owner, the poor widow. The lines describing him stress the splendour and reliability of his crowing – he is more accurate than a clock; his fine exterior; his pleasure in the retinue of seven hens who are 'his sustres and his paramours'. In the story we appreciate the cock's considerable learning as he explains to Pertelote why dreams should be taken seriously, although he is perhaps not as knowledgeable as he considers – he makes nonsense of the Latin '*In principio,/Mulier est hominis confusio*', a mistranslation of which (deliberate on Chaucer's part) would have been at once apparent to an educated audience. Chauntecleer is also capable of quick-thinking ingenuity, as he shows at the end of the poem when he outwits the fox by a display of cunning matching that of his captor. Chauntecleer, then, is a vigorous, commanding figure, with a gaze 'as it were a grym leoun', sure of his place in his little world and as 'roial as a prince is in an halle'. Yet this imperious figure could also be described as vain, foolish and ignorant – he is, after all, only a bird stalking around a farmyard. When he first spies the fox, instinct tells him to flee but he is seduced by the other's soothing flattery. Even though forewarned by the dream he is blind to the sinister double meaning in the fox's lines:

'My lord youre fader (God his soule blesse!)
And eek youre mooder, of hire gentillesse,
Han in myn hous y-been to my greet ese . . .'

Our hero presents himself, eyes closed (literally and metaphorically), a willing sacrifice to the fox's powers of deception. He deserves to be caught, just as later he deserves to escape because despite 'al his drede' he keeps a clear head and turns the tables on the fox. In addition to these specific examples of near-disastrous foolishness, there is something inherently absurd about the airs that Chauntecleer gives himself as he eagerly instructs his wife in dream-lore, or roams around his little kingdom, not deigning 'to sette his foot to grounde'. He has a very elevated and rather laughable idea of his own importance. Chaucer takes care to remind us from time to time that 'my tale is of a cok' – on the surface, it is not a *human* tragi-comedy, even if Chaucer's art and skill are such as to suggest that it almost might be.

It is often observed how the stories and story-tellers complement each other in *The Canterbury Tales*. In the *General Prologue* we learn nothing of the Nun's Priest: he is mentioned only in passing, together with two other priests who make up the Prioress's retinue. In the prologue to this tale Chaucer describes the teller as 'this sweete preest, this goodly man, Sir John', and the narrative he gives us reflects a tolerant and good-humoured individual. A few external details are supplied: the priest is mounted on a horse of poor quality ('foul and lene'); he is physically striking ('See, whiche braunes hath this gentil preest,' says the Host in the epilogue to the tale). We may surmise that his animal fable provides a humorous, secular version of his own life as a male priest surrounded by nuns, just as Chauntecleer is surrounded by his seven hens. If the Nun's Priest's hearers conclude that, because his hero the cock is told what to do and what not to do ('Dredeth no dreem' etc) by an unimaginatively practical female, the story-teller also must be at the mercy of an identical or similar female, in the shape of the Prioress . . . well, that is the conclusion they will draw. The Nun's Priest is canny enough not to say anything too explicit.

Humour and irony

The most obvious source of humour in this tale is the possession by the animals who are its principal characters of the power of speech and other human attributes. In fact, the humans in the story say nothing except for the shouts they utter in pursuit of the fox. This 'humanizing' of animals is a very old tradition in both written and spoken story-telling; a familiar modern example is George Orwell's *Animal Farm* (1945). Chaucer creates some simple humorous effects when he speaks of, say, Pertelote at one moment as if she were a fine lady, and the next reminds us that she is only a hen: we are told that she had conducted herself becomingly 'syn thilke day that she was seven night oold'. A loving compliment paid to her by Chauntecleer is similarly incongruous:

'For, whan I se the beautee of youre face,
Ye been so scarlet red aboute youre eyen,
It maketh al my drede for to dyen'

At one time the cock can assure his 'wife',

'By God, I hadde levere than my sherte
That ye hadde rad his legende, as have I.'

At another moment he is no more than a well-observed farm-yard animal, roaming up and down 'on his toos'. Beneath the animal exterior Chaucer packs various human qualities and failings: vanity and ostentation, argumentativeness, common sense, ingenuity, susceptibility to flattery. These attributes are played against external details of the animals' appearances or circumstances so that a comic tension is set up. Chaucer also capitalizes on our commonly-held beliefs about animal nature - Chauntecleer is a 'cocky' bird, while the fox obviously prides himself on his cunning.

The 'humanizing' of the animals is not restricted to the static possession of certain attributes but extends to the way in which the cock and hen debate as husband and wife might, or the manner in which Chauntecleer, having impressed upon Pertelote the importance of dreams, proceeds to take no notice of what he has himself been saying. We may recognize in this farmyard comedy elements of our own behaviour and responses and, of course, if the fable is to be instructive as well as entertaining, then it is necessary for us to see that the animal world is, in part, our human one. As the Nun's Priest suggests at the conclusion, those who consider the 'tale a folye' should 'taketh the moralite'.

We should not, however, assume an excessive weight of moral instruction in the story. The morals voiced by the Nun's Priest – beware of flattery, beware careless talk when you should keep silent – these are apt enough but scarcely original. Chaucer juggles with some ideas which preoccupied the medieval mind, such as predestination and the significance of dreams, but no conclusions are reached and the story-teller shows no sign of wanting to subject such ideas to any tough analysis. There is a playful element in such discussions. In any case the context in which these concerns are raised – the fate of a cock – must make us doubtful of the author's seriousness. Pertelote's 'scientific' explanation of her husband's bad dream is partly an exposition of the important medieval theory of 'humours'; yet this is followed by her advice that he should cure himself by a diet of worms and herbal laxatives. The animal remedy incongruously jostles the human debate. The Nun's Priest lists some of the conflicting schools of thought on the subject of predestination – and then says he cannot understand them. Serious subjects are treated lightly, just as, in reverse, events which would not generally be considered of much significance – the tribulations of some farmyard birds – are dealt with by the narrator as if they were matters of historic importance. Our uncertainty about exactly how far we are to take the story-teller seriously is paralleled by our uncertainty about the status of the beasts in the *Tale*: are they animals dressed up as human beings, or humans disguised as animals?

As already indicated above, the author changes his focus, so that he sometimes treats his characters as animals, sometimes as people, without allowing them to remain long in one category. He exploits the gap between the human and the animal by the ironic device of the 'mock-heroic'. This technique gives to an insignificant event or circumstance aspects of grandeur and epic importance so that the original event becomes inflated far out of proportion and, in the very absurdity of heroic exaggeration, can be more clearly seen as ridiculous or trivial. The best-known example of a sustained piece of mock-heroic in English literature is Pope's poem *The Rape of the Lock* (1714), in which the illicit cutting-off of a lock of lady's hair is the trivial motive for an elaborate epic 'battle'. The most obvious example of the mock-heroic in *The Nun's Priest's Tale* occurs near the end when the uproar among the hens is compared to the lamentation of women when Troy was captured. Pertelote herself shrieks:

'Ful louder than dide Hasdrubales wyf,
Whan that hir housbonde hadde lost his lyf
And that the Romayns hadde brend Cartage –'

Such comparisons between historic events and the happenings in a farmyard are found elsewhere. The imminent death of Chauntecleer is likened to the death of Richard I. The dream stories that Chauntecleer recounts to prove his point to a sceptical wife are to do with violence and sudden death, events of historical, Biblical, *human* significance. It is easy to lose sight of the fact – and it is a fact we are meant to lose sight of in our absorption in the story – that the potential 'tragedy' of *The Nun's Priest's Tale* is no more than the capture of a bird by a natural predator.

When the narrator says that the hens cried out:

'As, whan that Nero brende the citee
of Rome, cryden the senatoures wyves,
For that hir husbondes losten alle hir lyves'

he is bringing together a chorus of hens and a group of lamenting women. The effect is to belittle the farmyard disturbance. By pretending to elevate it to – even above – the level of some distant human catastrophe, the author diminishes rather than enlarges the significance of the animal turmoil. Nevertheless, in the ironic, mock-heroic process something of the grandeur or scale of the comparison may rub off onto the trivial event or circumstance that occasioned it. Although the fuss about Chauntecleer's disappearance is, on one level, absurd, in the context of farm life his capture is a disastrous loss for the hens, as it would no doubt have been a blow to the careful housekeeping of the 'sely widwe and . . . hir doghtres two'.

The world of the farmyard is enclosed, literally ('with stikkes and a drye dych withoute') and metaphorically; it is so limited that Chauntecleer can behave like a king, though his domain is no more than a patch of earth, because he is ignorant of the reality outside. The reality of that wider world is most malignantly represented by the fox in the grove of trees. The storyteller recreates for us the tiny kingdom under the rule of the cock, then juxtaposes it ironically with the impoverished quarters of the widow. In turn, references throughout the poem introduce the larger world of history, business, human affairs and disasters, all of which place the farmyard in a more distant perspective. Yet the animal inhabitants of that farmyard are satisfied with themselves, believe that what surrounds them is the whole world, just as, for us, our surroundings constitute our 'world'. It is, finally, not Chauntecleer's pretensions to knowledge and mastery that are being (gently) mocked in the course of the poem so much as the human variety.

Dreams and predestination

These two topics form the basis for lengthy digressions, together taking up more than a third of the *Tale*. Medieval speculation, as reflected in this poem, divided dreams into those which, either in disguised or in plain form, gave some glimpse of the future and those which had no such significance but proceeded from an imbalance of elements in the body. The first type might be described as coming to the dreamer from outside, the granting of some truth, vision or warning; the second rises from within the sleeper. Chauntecleer adheres to the first interpretation, Pertelote to the second. Chaucer often uses dreams in his poetry and the subject was evidently of great intrinsic interest to him as well as an artistically useful means of enlarging a narrative. Within the context of *The Nun's Priest's Tale*, we can see that he supports Chauntecleer's point of view; the cock is right to be afraid. But the whole debate is somewhat deflated by the fact that the hero, though stout in defence of his theory, fails to act upon what he believes.

Predestination is the name for the doctrine which holds that an individual's life is laid down in advance by God or destiny and that this preordained pattern cannot be changed. If God is considered to be all-knowing (as He must be, otherwise He would not be God), then He must know what we are to do in the future. Does such foreknowledge imply that we are bound to do what it is foreseen we will do? In other words, is human freedom of choice restricted – even abolished? Are the choices which we imagine we are making on our own initiative already predetermined for us? Such questions preoccupied medieval thinkers. The Nun's Priest touches upon them but then shies nervously away from them – he claims to be concerned with telling nothing more than an everyday story of the farmyard. Perhaps Chaucer is here amusing himself with the gap between the theoretical and the practical: academics may argue about predestination and its impact on humanity but their theories make no difference to day to day life. Thus it does not matter whether it was destined or not for Chauntecleer to be captured by the fox – the important facts are that he has been caught and must escape before being eaten!

Chaucer's verse

Chaucer's verse is flexible and varied. It encompasses straight-forward description (see the opening of the *Tale* for an example), simple narrative (see the two stories of the travellers recounted by Chauntecleer), rhetorical flourishes and the re-creation of mood or action.

For an example of the *rhetorical flourish or aside*, look at the outburst on the subject of murder:

'O blisful God, that art so just and trewe,
Lo! how that thou biwreyest mordre alway.
Mordre wol out, that se we day by day;
Mordre is so wlatsom and abhomynable
To God. . .'

It is obvious that this kind of comment does not further the story or impart information but rather serves as a vehicle for the speaker's indignation (the exclamation 'Lo!', and the stressed repetitions of 'mordre' suggest this). It occurs near the climax of Chauntecleer's first dream-narrative and stands in contrast to the unadorned story which surrounds it. Such asides are com-monplace in Chaucer and are composed in accordance with various rhetorical rules. Other examples are the passage con-demning the 'false mordrour' (460–63) and the ironic appeals to Venus and to 'Gaufred' (576–88).

A fine instance of Chaucer's ability to contain action in verse is *the description* of the farmyard uproar. Each line presents us with a self-contained picture or sound but the effect is cumulative:

'They (the animals) yolleden as feendes doon in helle;
The dokes cryden as men wolde hem quelle;
The gees for feere flowen over the trees;
Out of the hyve cam the swarm of bees. . .'

Alliteration and *onomatopoeia* are used in the re-creation of the noises made by the humans in the chase (632–35). Variety of effect keeps our attention; it is also a measure of the writer's mastery.

Grammar, pronunciation and versification

Chaucer's language, sometimes called Middle English, represents a transitional stage between Old English (or Anglo-Saxon) and what we speak today. By Chaucer's time English had become a blend of Saxon and the French brought across at the time of the Norman Conquest, but there were distinct dialects in different areas of the country (stronger than modern regional variations). Chaucer's own dialect was the East Midland and, largely because this was the variation of English used in court and government, it was this form of the language that became the standard one. Chaucer's English is recognizably close to us – perhaps closer than might at first sight appear – but there are differences in vocabulary and in the way words work. Such differences are no real barrier to understanding and enjoying Chaucer: the sense of the verse can usually be appreciated without precise grammatical knowledge and it can sometimes be helpful to pronounce aloud an unfamiliar-looking word, the meaning of which may be more apparent in its sound than in its spelling. The latter, incidentally, was not regularized in Chaucer's day, and the same word may be differently spelled in different parts of the text. Middle English was more strongly inflected than its modern counterpart, that is, there was greater variation in the endings of words. For example, where in modern English only the third person singular of the present tense is inflected ('makes', 'falls') in Middle English we find a number of variations to verb-endings in the present tense ('make, makest, maketh, maken).

These very brief notes on grammar may be helpful:

Noun inflection is very similar to what we are used to in modern English:

-es is almost invariably the mark of the possessive (genitive) case, e.g. 'mannes herte', 'preestes sone', and (e)s indicates the plural, e.g. 'hennes', 'bookes', 'humours'. There are a few exceptions to the standard possessive inflection, e.g. 'fader kin' means 'father's family'.

There are also irregular plurals, mostly familiar ones ('wommen', 'oxen'), a few not ('eyen').

Pronouns: it should be noted that there is no equivalent for 'its' in Middle English. 'His' is used for persons and things, e.g. 'the sonne in his ascencioun'. 'Hir' means both 'her' and 'their', but the context generally makes clear which is intended.

Sometimes the pronoun 'thou' is attached to the verb in a question, e.g. 'woldestow' meaning 'would you'.

The plural of 'that' is 'tho', not 'those'.

Verbs: changes between tenses are not dissimilar to those in modern English. Note that the past participle form of a verb is frequently indicated by the prefix y-, e.g. 'yseyled', 'ywarned'.

Adverbs: in modern English almost all adverbs end '-ly'. This was one of the endings used in Chaucer's day but we also find adverbs ending in '-e' and '-liche'.

Pronunciation

Short vowels

In words of English origin

'a' pronounced like 'a' in French *placer*; but not like 'a' in English 'cat'.

'e' pronounced like 'e' in Modern English 'men'.

'i' pronounced like 'i' in 'pin'. 'y' is often written for 'i', and has the same sound as 'i'.

'o' pronounced like 'o' in 'not'. Before letters written with a number of short strokes, like 'm, n,' and especially a combination of these two, 'o' is written for 'u', but should be pronounced like 'u', as for example, in 'comen, love, somer, monk'.

'u' pronounced like 'u' in 'pull', or like 'oo' in 'soot'; but not like 'u' in 'duke'.

Long vowels

It is often possible to recognize a long vowel by its being duplicated in writing. For example 'taak' contains a long 'a'; 'sooth' contains a long 'o'.

'a' pronounced like 'a' in 'father'.

'e' pronounced like 'e' acute or like 'e' grave in French. Only a knowledge of the origin of the words in Old English can guide the reader to distinguish between the close and open sounds, as they are called, in Chaucer; but the former sound is usually represented in Modern English by 'ee', and the latter by 'ea'. Modern English 'need' had a close vowel in Old English, where it was spelt 'nēd'; Modern English 'mead', a meadow, was 'mēd' in Old English with an open vowel. As an indication that these two vowels had distinct sounds, we may note that Chaucer very rarely makes them rhyme.

'i' (often written 'y'), pronounced like 'ee' in 'feel'.

'o' pronounced either like 'o' in 'so', or like 'a' in 'call'. Chaucer recognizes the different pronunciations just as he distinguishes the two long 'e' sounds. In Modern English the former sound is represented by 'oo', as in 'soon' while the latter is like the vowel sound in 'note'.

'u' pronounced like 'oo' in 'soon'.

Diphthongs

'ai, ei, ay', and 'ey' (pronounced like the diphthong in 'day', though some authorities believe they were sounded like 'i' in 'line'.

'au, aw' pronounced like 'ou' in 'house'; but not before the combination '-ght' like the 'o' in 'not'.

'eu, ew' pronounced like 'ew' in 'few'.

'oi, oy' pronounced like 'oy' in 'boy'.

'ou, ow' pronounced like 'u', or like 'au, aw'.

In words of French origin

Such of these words as had already become part and parcel of the everyday speech would obey the rules for the pronunciation of English vowel sounds; the others would retain the vowels of the French language, which were sounded much as they are today.

In unaccented syllables

The final '-e' so common at the end of a line and elsewhere is sounded like the second syllable of the word 'china'.

Consonants

The consonants had generally the same pronunciation as they have today, with certain slight modifications.

There were no silent consonants, unless, as some scholars believe, the 'g' before 'n' is not sounded.

'kn' is pronounced as in modern German.

'gg' is pronounced like the 'dge' in modern English 'ridge'.

'gh' as in modern German may be either palatal or guttural, according to whether it is preceded by a palatal or a guttural vowel.

'ng' is sounded as in southern English 'fin-ger', not as in 'sing-er'.

'th' (initial) is sounded as in 'thin', not as in 'then'.

'ch' in words of both English and French origin is pronounced like the 'ch' of modern English 'choose'.

'w' before 'r' is pronounced like a rapidly sounded 'oo'.

'h' in words of French origin and in words like 'he, him', which are rarely emphasized, is silent; but in most words of English origin an initial 'h' is sounded. Where the metre demands that a final '-e' should be elided before an 'h', that 'h' is silent.

Final 'f' is sounded as 'f', and not as 'v'.

Final 's' is sounded as 's', and not as 'z'.

Chaucer's use of the final -e

It is important to say something about the function of the final -e found at the end of many words in Chaucer's verse. At the beginning of the fourteenth century these were generally sounded as separate syllables, but by the end of the century they were coming into disuse. In Chaucer's verse the final -e may represent an inflexional change in a noun, an adjective, or a verb; or it may be what is left of a word-ending in Old English. There are many explanations of this termination, and the following rules usually apply in Chaucer.

1 The final -e is usually sounded, except when
(a) it is slurred over before a word beginning with a vowel (e.g. Of deerne love he koude and of solas): before certain words beginning with 'h'; any part of the verb to have (e.g. a clerkhadde litherly biset his while); the adverbs heer, how, and a silent 'h' as in honour, him and hem (e.g. For for no cry hir maide koudehim calle).
(b) it is sometimes dropped in some words in common use as were, wolde.

2 The final -e should always be sounded at the end of a line.

Versification

In his earlier works Chaucer had used the eight-syllabled line commonly found in French poets of the period. In the *Canterbury Tales*, however, he sometimes employs the ten-syllabled line, rhyming in couplets. This is his metre throughout the *Nun's Priest's Tale*. As the line is somewhat long, he made use of a break, the caesura, in the middle of the line, that is after the fifth syllable, but as such a break in every case at the same point would make for a rigidity which would not be in keeping with the easy style of this tale, and of some others, we find the break in other positions. Lines 55–64 give examples of this change of position. Lines 55 and 57 are true to pattern: 58 shows the caesura after the third syllable, 59 after the fourth, 61 after the sixth, and 64 after the seventh. Elsewhere we shall find examples of lines eleven syllables long, but in counting syllables up we must remember that a final -e is very often elided, before a following vowel, or an -h. Line 55 has eleven syllables, for the final -e is sounded throughout at the end of a line. An -ed, or -es is usually sounded as a separate syllable; the endings -ioun or -ience are also dissyllables, as in lines 348 and 60. Sometimes the line has only nine syllables; examples will be found in lines 620 and 194. Chaucer is not strict about the sounding of final -e in every case. Bear this point in mind when you are counting up syllables.

You will notice a device of Chaucer's whereby he prevents the narrative from being disjointed: he begins a new paragraph very frequently with the second line of the couplet. Many instances of this practice can be found; for instance, in lines 284, 320, 344, but where a more definite change of subject is to be marked, the new paragraph begins with the first line, e.g. 391, 449, 501.

General questions

1 Why is the poor widow introduced into the *Tale*?

Guideline notes for an answer

Not a character in her own right, no name or physical description provided by story-teller. She is reflected in the meagreness of her smallholding – 'litel was hir catel and hir rente' – and the simplicity of her way of life – can't afford self-indulgence. Defined as much by what she doesn't have as by what she does: no more than three sows, no wine on her table, no appetizing sauce for her food, no chance of over-eating. Despite narrowness of her life she is contented, has 'hertes suffisaunce', lives 'in pacience' and manages to provide for herself and two daughters by 'housbandrie of swich as God hire sente'. Principal function of this character is to be placed ironically as counterpart to Chauntecleer. Where widow lives poorly, he leads expansive life, a prince in his own domain. Where colours associated with widow are plain opposites (her table is provided with white and black, i.e. 'milk and broun breed') the cock is endowed with a fine array (see lines 93–8). Where she lives in contented widowhood, withdrawn from sexual relations, Chauntecleer has his ample harem of seven hens. Further temperamental contrast: where old woman is long-suffering, in good health because of simple way of life, etc. the bird in her farmyard is anxious, vulnerable, troubled by dreams and fears. Over-riding irony here – it's the human owner who lives in peace and plain surroundings while domestic farmyard creatures appear to live more 'splendid' (and more troubled) existence. Appearance of widow also 'frames' the story: she and her two daughters appear at beginning and end, during chase after fox, and remind us of wider world surrounding self-absorption of Chauntecleer and Pertelote.

2 Describe, with examples, the human characteristics Chaucer gives to Chauntecleer.

3 'Pertelote is very much more than a mere hen.' Do you consider this comment justified?

4 'The farmyard world is restricted but it is one in which all the essential human emotions are to be discovered.' Do you agree?

5 Discuss the part played by dreams in *The Nun's Priest's Tale*.

6 'Animals dressed up as human beings or humans disguised as animals.' Which is the better description of the characters in this story?

7 What picture of medieval life do we gain from *The Nun's Priest's Tale*?

8 Discuss, with examples from the text, the use of the mock-heroic in the poem.

9 What interest do the Priest's digressions add to the *Tale*?

10 'By setting his scene in a farmyard, Chaucer reduces everything to the same flippant level.' How would you answer this charge?

11 By what means does Chaucer remind us that it is a priest who is telling this story?

12 How does the Nun's Priest maintain the interest of his listeners in what he has to say?

13 At the conclusion of *The Nun's Priest's Tale*, the story-teller draws certain 'lessons' or 'morals' from what has happened. What are they and how far do they provide a fitting conclusion to the Tale?

14 Why should we still read *The Nun's Priest's Tale*? What is there of interest for the modern reader?

15 Discuss and illustrate the range of Chaucer's verse.

16 'A very simple story which cannot support the asides and interruptions which surround it.' How far do you agree?

17 Would you agree that vanity is the principal human failing attacked in the story?

18 Write a dialogue for Chauntecleer and Pertelote that might plausibly follow the cock's escape and return to the farm. Remember that each bird may have reason to change his/her opinions.

19 'Light in tone, serious in purpose.' How far is this a justifiable comment on *The Nun's Priest's Tale*?

20 What different types of humour do you find in the poem?

Further reading

The Canterbury Tales translated by Nevil Coghill (Penguin, 1951)

For Chaucer's life and material on *The Canterbury Tales* as a whole see:
An Introduction to Chaucer Hussey, Spearing and Winny (CUP, 1965)
Chaucer's World ed. Hussey (CUP)
The Life and Times of Geoffrey Chaucer John Gardner (Cape, 1977)

For material on *The Nun's Priest's Tale* see:
New Pelican Guide to English Literature: Medieval Literature Part One (Penguin, 1982). This contains a helpful essay by David Holbrook on the poem.

An Introduction to Chaucer Derek Brewer (Longman, 1984)

Glossary

Note: Chaucer uses *i* and *y* as equivalents; *ou* and *ow* are inter-changeable; as are *-ey-* and *-ay-* (which may also be writen *-ei-* or *-ai-*).

The student is advised to consult the Textual notes in association with this Glossary.

abhomynable *hateful, unnatural.*
above *above, upwards.*
aboute *about.*
abrayde *woke suddenly, with a start.*
abyde *remain, wait.*
accord *musical harmony.*
accordant *in keeping with, proportioned to.*
actes *records, histories.*
adversitee *ill-fortune, mishap.*
aferd *afraid, frightened.*
afferme *assert the truth of.*
affrayed *frightened, afraid.*
afright *terrified.*
after *according to* (l.469); *afterwards* (l.360).
agaste *terrify* (l. 322); *terrified.*
agayn *towards* (l. 503); *back.*
agon *gone, past.*
agrief *unkindly, as a grievance.*
agu *ague.*
al *quite.*
al-be-it *although.*
alday *continually.*
als *also.*
also *as.*
altercacioun *disputing, wrangling.*
alway *always.*
amended *improved, bettered.*
anhanged *hanged.*
anighte *in the night.*
anon *straightaway, at once.*
anoye *displease, weary.*
ape *ape.*

apoplexie *apoplexy, loss of sensation in the head.*
apothecarie *apothecary, one who sells drugs.*
areest *seizure, arrest.*
argument *formal proof, as in logic.*
aright *favourably, to my advantage.*
arrayed *ordered, disposed.*
arresten *stop.*
arwe *arrow.*
arys *arise from bed.*
as *as regards.*
as *pray* (see note to l. 177).
ascenscioun *ascension, rising above the horizon.*
asure *azure, sky blue.*
atones *at once.*
attame *open, begin.*
atte *at the.*
attempre *temperate, moderate.*
auctorite *authority.*
auctour *author, authority.*
aungel *angel.*
availle *avail, influence a decision.*
avauntour *boaster, braggart.*
aventure *luck, fate, chance.*
avisioun *vision, dream.*
avoy *alas.*
await *ambush.*
bad *bade, commanded, instructed.*
bak *back.*
bane *death, destruction.*
bar *bore, conducted.*
bataille *battle, fight.*

batailled *embattled, battlemented, crenellated.*
be *been* (l. 33).
bee *be* (l. 225).
been *be* (l. 92).
beer *carried.*
beest *beast, animal.*
beme *perch, beam, roost.*
beme *trumpet.*
bene *bean, trifling article.*
benedicitee *God bless us.*
benefice *benefice, living.*
berd *beard.*
bere *bear.*
beryis *berries.*
berkynge *barking.*
bete *beat, flap.*
beth pl. of *be.*
betwixe *between.*
bifel *happened, chanced.*
biforn *before.*
bigan *to begin.*
bigyle *cheat, fool, trick.*
biknewe *confessed.*
biwaille *lament, complain of.*
biwreye *reveal.*
blak *black.*
blisful *blessed, happy, joyful.*
blisse *blessedness, bliss.*
blithe *merry, cheerful.*
bole *bull.*
boold *bold.*
boon *bone.*
bord *table.*
boterflye *butterfly.*
botme *bottom.*
bour *bedroom, bower.*
box *boxwood.*
brak see **breek.**
brast *burst, broke.*
breed *bread.*
breek *break.*
bren *bran, husk.*
brend *burnt, sacked.*
brende *burnt.*
brid *bird.*
broghte *brought.*

brouke *enjoy the use of.*
bulte *sift.*
burned *burnished.*
but *unless.*
butiller *butler.*
by *nearby, beside.*
byde *wait.*
byle *bill, beak.*
bynethe *beneath, downwards.*
cas *incident, circumstance, misfortune.*
caste *lifted up* (l. 427); *resolved, intended* (l. 309).
casuelly *by accident.*
catel *property, wealth, possessions cattle* (l. 61).
centaure *the herb centaury.*
certes *truly, assuredly, certainly.*
certeyn *definite* (l. 302); *certainly* (l. 551).
chaf *chaff, husks.*
chapitre *chapter of a book.*
cherl *churl, peasant, rustic.*
chide *reprove, find fault with.*
chirche *church.*
choys *choice, liberty to choose.*
chuk *'chuk', the cry made to call the attention of poultry.*
chukke *to make the cry of 'chuk', as above.*
clappe *to talk:* lit., *to make the sound of the clapper of a bell.*
clepe *cry, call, name.*
clerk *learned man, scholar, a student of philosophy.*
clokke *a mechanical clock, as distinct from a sundial.*
clomben *risen, ascended, climbed, mounted.*
cloos *closed, shut tight.*
clos *enclosure, garden, yard.*
cok *cock.*
cold *baneful, disastrous.*
colera *choler, one of the four humours.*
coleryk *choleric, possessing choler in excess.*

colfox *a fox with black markings, a brant-fox.*

commune *common, the same way.*

compaignable *friendly, companionable.*

compaignye *company.*

comparisoun *comparison.*

compleccioun *temperament, resulting from mixture of humours.*

compleet *complete, finished.*

compleyne *lament, mourn.*

comynge *coming, visit.*

condicioneel *conditional, provisional.*

congregacioun *crowd, large assembly, number.*

conseil *advice* (l. 487); *secrets* (l. 522).

conseille *advise, give advice.*

contek *strife with bloodshed.*

contrarie *opposite, enemy, natural foe.*

contree *country.*

coomen *came.*

corn *a grain of corn, seed.*

cotage *cottage.*

cote *cottage.*

countrefete *imitate, equal, rival.*

cours *voyage, course, journey.*

coward *coward.*

crew *crowed.*

cride *cried out.*

cronycle *record, history, chronicle.*

curteys *courtly, gracious, courteous.*

damoysele *damsel, mistress.*

dar *dare.*

daun *sir, lord, master.*

dawenynge *dawn, daybreak.*

debonaire *gracious, kindly, gentle.*

dede *dead.*

dede *deed.*

deed *dead.*

deel *portion, bit, part.*

deere *dear.*

deign *it pleased.*

delit *delight.*

delyverly *deftly, cleverly, quickly.*

departen *separate, part company.*

desport *amusement.*

devel *devil, demon.*

devyse *set forth, describe.*

deye *dairy-woman.*

deye *die.*

deyntee *choice, rare.*

dide *exerted* (l. 578).

diete *food, diet.*

diffye *mistrust, denounce.*

digestyves *medicines to help digestion, foods to help.*

discrecioun *good judgment, tact, skill.*

discreet *tactful, wise.*

disese *discomfort, cause of distress.*

disputisoun *controversy, debate, argument.*

dissymulour *deceiver, dissembler.*

divyne *guess, suspect.*

do *do, cause* (l. 664).

doctour *teacher, learned doctor.*

doctrine *instruction, learning.*

doghtor *daughter.*

doke *duck.*

donge *dung.*

donge *manure.*

dore *door.*

dorste *durst, dared.*

doutelees *unhesitatingly, doubtless.*

drecched *distressed, tortured.*

drede *terror, fear.*

drede *to fear, to be feared.*

dreynt *drowned.*

dwelle *tarry, delay, linger.*

dych *ditch.*

dyde *died, see* **deye**.

dystaf *dystaff.*

ech *each.*

eeris *ears.*

eet see **ete**.

effect *fulfilment.*

eke *also.*

ellebor *hellebore.*

elles *otherwise, else.*

enclosed *enclosed.*

endite *express in writing, set down.*

enduren *endure, experience.*

engendren *to arise, originate.*

engyned *racked, tortured.*

ensample *example, instance.*

entente *intention, purpose, motive.*

equynoxial *celestial equator.*

er *before.*

erly *early.*

erst *before.*

eschewed *avoided, escaped.*

ese *ease, comfort, happiness, content.*

espyen *espy, detect, observe.*

estaat *state, condition.*

ete *eat, devour.*

everemo *ever more, always.*

everichon *every one, one and all.*

experience *actual experience.*

expowen *made clear, explained.*

ey *egg.*

eylen *afflict, befall.*

fader *father.*

faire *beautiful, gracefully, well.*

falle *happen, betide, chance.*

faren *gone.*

faste *relentlessly, volubly, quickly.*

fayn *willingly, gladly, joyfully.*

feelynge *taste, musical feeling.*

feend *devil, fiend.*

feere *sudden dread, fear.*

feith *faith, very truth.*

felawe *comrade, companion, friend.*

felonye *crime.*

fer *far.*

fevere *fever.*

fil *befel, occurred.*

flaterye *flattery.*

flatour *flatterer.*

flaugh *flown.*

flee *fly.*

fly *flew.*

flour *flower.*

flowen *flew.*

folye *foolish piece, silly tale.*

fond, foond *found.*

for *because of* (l. 31); *because* (l. 548); *against* (l. 351).

forncast *preordained, foreseen.*

fors *heed, count.*

forslewthen *lose by idleness, or sloth.*

forthermore *moreover, further.*

forwityng *foreknowledge, previous knowledge.*

forwoot *foreknows.*

foul *dirty, unkempt, ill-groomed.*

fourty *forty.*

free *carefree, generous.*

freend *friend.*

fro *from.*

ful *much* (l. 172); *very* (l. 60).

fume *vapours, arising from indigestion.*

fumetere *fumitory, the name of a plant.*

fy *fie, for shame.*

fyn *finest, excellent, choice.*

fynde *find.*

fyr *fire.*

gabbe *boast, lie, speak wildly.*

gaitris *buckthorn.*

gan *began* (if used with *to*); *did*, as an auxiliary.

game *sport, fun.*

gape *open the mouth in death.*

gargat *throat.*

gees *geese.*

gentil *high-born, noble.*

gentillesse *high-birth, courtesy, kindness.*

gesse *guess, suppose.*

gilt *guilt, sin.*

glad *happy, merry.*

glade *gladden.*

gladly *eagerly, happily.*

glowynge *glowing.*

go *walk.* In line 86: *sound, are played.*

goute *gout.*

governance *control, self-control.*

grace *good fortune, sign of favour.*

graunt *great, much.*

greet *great.*

gretteste *greatest.*

greve *grove of trees.*

grone *groan.*
grote *fourpenny-piece, groat.*
grym *fierce.*
ha ha *a cry of alarm.*
habundant *abundant, excessive.*
halle *hall, living room.*
han *have.*
happe *happen.*
hardy *bold, strong, venturesome.*
harrow *a cry for help.*
haste *haste.*
hath see **han.**
haven *harbour, haven.*
heed *head.*
heeld p.t. of **holden**: *hold.*
heele *healing, health.*
heere *hear.*
heere *here.*
heeris *hairs.*
heet *called, named.*
hegge *hedge.*
heigh *high.*
heighe *high.*
hele *cover, hide, conceal.*
hem *them.*
hente *seize.*
herbe *herb.*
herbergage *accommodation, lodgings, shelter.*
herbeyve *herbive, buck's horn.*
here *hear.*
herkne *hark, listen to.*
herte *heart.*
hertelees *coward.*
hevene *heaven, the heavens.*
hevynesse *sadness, sorrow.*
hewe *hue, colour.*
hewed *coloured.*
highte *called.*
hir, hire *their.*
hir, hire *her, hers.*
hire *herself.*
hirselven *herself.*
hogg *hog, pig.*
holden *consider, reckon, esteem.*
homycides *murderers.*
hoo *stop!.*

hoold *keeping, safekeeping.*
hooly *holy, pure, innocent.*
hoote *hot.*
hostelrie *inn, hotel.*
hostiler *landlord, innkeeper.*
hosten *to be called, to be named; command, promise.*
hound *hound, dog.*
housbonde *husband.*
housbondrie *economy.*
howp *whoop.*
humour see note to l. 159.
hyder *hither.*
hydous *hideous, hateful, frightful.*
hye see **heigh.**
hym *him.*
in *inn.*
iniquitee *wickedness, guile.*
jade *wretched nag, poor horse.*
jangle *babble, chatter, talk idly.*
jape *mockery, illusions.*
jeet *jet.*
jolif *happy, cheerful, carefree.*
joye *joy, happiness.*
just *just, fair.*
kan *can, am able.*
katapuce *catapuce.*
keen *cows, kine.*
keep *notice, care, heed.*
kepe *guard, protect, shield.*
knok *knock, blow.*
konne see **kan.**
koude *could.*
kyn *kin, family, lineage.*
kynde *instinct, nature.*
lak *shortage, lack.*
large *ample, bounteous.*
lat *allow, permit.*
latter *later, final.*
lawriol *spurge laurel.*
leere *learn, teach yourself.*
legende *legend, story of a saint.*
legge *leg.*
leme *flame.*
lenger *longer.*
leoun *lion.*
lese *lose.*

leste *it pleased.*
lette *hinder, delay, prevent.*
leve *leave, departure.*
leve *leave.*
levere *rather, preferably.*
leye *bet, wager.*
lief *dear.*
liggen *lie in ambush.*
lightly *quickly, rapidly.*
liste *it pleased.*
lite *little, short time.*
litel *little, scanty.*
lith *limb.*
lith see **lye.**
logge *lodging, roosting place.*
logged *accommodated.*
loggyng *lodgings, billet.*
loken p.p. of to lock; *held fast.*
lond *land, field.*
looke *see, take care, consider.*
loore *kind of knowledge, instruction, advice.*
lorn *lost.*
losengeour *deceiver, flatterer.*
losten *lost.*
loude *loudly.*
lust *pleasure, desire, inclination.*
lye *speak falsely, lie, deceive.*
lye *lie down, rest.*
lyf *life.*
lyk *like, resembling.*
lylye *lily.*
lyte *little, small.*
lyves see **lyf.**
maad *made.*
maister *master.*
maistow contracted from *mayest thou.*
maked *made.*
malencolye *melancholy, black bile.*
man *one,* used impersonally.
maner *kind of, sort of.*
mateere *matter, subject.*
maugree *in spite of.*
may *may, can.*
maze *muddled fancy, delusive thought.*

me *me.*
meel *meal, repast.*
men *one,* used to form the passive.
mente *meant, intended.*
mercy *thanks.*
mermayde *mermaid.*
mervaille *marvel, wonder.*
mery *pleasant, cheerful.*
meschaunce *misfortune, mishap, disaster.*
meschief *trouble, difficulty.*
messe *mass.*
met *dreamed.*
mette see **met.**
meynee *following, mob, company.*
ministre *officer, responsible official.*
moost *mostly, usually.*
moot *may, must.*
moralite *moral, lesson.*
mordre *murder.*
mordred *murdered.*
mordrour *murderer.*
morwe *morning.*
morwenynge *morning.*
moste see **moot,** *had to.*
muche *much.*
multiply *people, increase.*
murie *merry;* see **mery,** also **myrie.**
myddel *midst.*
myrthe *something cheerful, merriment.*
namo, namoore *no more.*
narwe *small, confined.*
nas *was not.*
nat *not.*
natheless *nevertheless.*
nature *nature, instinct.*
natureelly *by instinct, naturally.*
nayle *nail, claw.*
ne *not* (l. 71); *nor* (l. 150).
neded *needed, was needful.*
nedely *of necessity, necessarily.*
nedes *necessarily.*
neer *nearer, closer.*
nekke *neck.*

nere *were it not.*
nevere *never.*
newe *new, recent, recently.*
noght *not at all.*
nones *occasion.*
nonne *nun.*
noon *none, no, not any.*
noot *knows not.*
norice *nurse, attendant.*
notabilitee *a thing worthy of note.*
nothyng *not at all, by no means.*
noys *noise, hubbub.*
ny *near.*
nyce *foolish, weak.*
nygard *niggard, mean person.*
nyght *night.*
nys *is not.*
o *one.*
of *concerning* (l. 563); *by* (l. 382); *in* (l. 84).
ofter *oftener, more.*
on *concerning.*
ones *once.*
oold *old.*
oon see **o.**
oonly *only.*
oother *other.*
orgon *organ.*
orlogge *clock.*
out *come out!, help!*
outsterte *rushed out.*
outrely *utterly, completely, entirely.*
owene *own.*
owle *owl.*
paramour *lover.*
pardee *by God, assuredly.*
parfit *perfect.*
passe *pass on* (l. 173); *surpass* (l. 545).
pasture *act of feeding.*
peer *equal.*
pees *peace.*
pekke *peck, pick.*
peple *people.*
perilous *dangerous, ill-omened.*
peyne *pain, torment, anguish, distress.*

peyne *to take pains, exert oneself.*
phisik *medicine.*
pitous *pitiable.*
plesaunce *pleasure, will.*
plesen *please.*
pleye *amuse, to jest.*
pleyne *bewail, mourn, lament.*
point *detail.*
poure *poor.*
poweer *power, ability.*
poynaunt *piquant, pungent, sharp.*
powpe *toot, blow, puff.*
preeste *priest.*
preeve *proof, test.*
present *present.*
preye *pray, beg.*
prisoun *prison.*
prively *secretly.*
propertee *quality, power, property.*
prow *benefit, advantage, profit, well-being.*
pryde *pride, self-esteem.*
pryme *nine o'clock in the morning.*
purge *purge.*
pyne *tortured, tormented, racked.*
quelle *kill.*
quod *quoth, said.*
rad see **rede.**
rage *frenzy.*
ravysshed *delighted, overcome.*
real *regal, royal, majestic, kingly.*
recche *interpret, expound.*
recchelees *heedless, regardless.*
rede *red.*
rede *read.*
reed *red.*
rekke *care, trouble, mind.*
regioun *place, region.*
reme *kingdom, realm.*
remedie *remedy.*
remenant *remainder, rest.*
rennen *run, hurry.*
renoun *reputation, fame.*
rente *income.*
rente *was torn.*
repaire *retire, betake oneself.*
repleccioun *over-eating, excess.*

repleet *over-full.*
report *relate, tell.*
resonable *equitable, just, fair.*
rethor *orator, writer.*
reulen *govern, control, rule.*
revel *joy, merriment.*
reverence *respect, honour.*
revers *contrary, opposite.*
rewe impers., *saddens, fills with regret.*
right *quite, exactly, precisely, even.*
roghte see **rekke.**
roial *royal.*
rome *strut, stalk.*
ronne see **rennan.**
roore *shout, bellow, cry out.*
rude *rough, broad, unrefined.*
ryde *ride.*
saille *sail.*
saufly *safely, with confidence.*
saugh *seen.*
say p.t. **se.**
sayn see **seye.**
scarlet *scarlet.*
scole *university, 'the schools'.*
scorne *ridicule.*
se *see.*
secree *secret, reserved.*
see *sea.*
seinte *holy, blessed.*
seith *say.*
seken *search.*
sely *simple, innocent.*
sente *sent.*
sentence *matter, meaning, judgement, sense, sentiment.*
sette *consider worth, account worth.*
sewe *pursue, follow.*
seye *say.*
seyle *sail.*
seyn *saw.*
seynd *grilled, toasted.*
shal (also **shul**) *shall.*
shaltow *shalt thou.*
shende *harm, punish, confuse.*
sherte *shirt of mail.*
sholde *should.*

shoon *shone.*
shortly *in short, in a few words.*
shot *a missile.*
shrewe *curse.*
shrighte *shrieked.*
signe *astronomical sign of the zodiac.*
significatioun *sign, forewarning.*
sik *sick, ill.*
siker *sure, reliable.*
sikerly *certainly, surely, confidently.*
singen see **syngen.**
sire *sir.*
sith *since.*
sklendre *frugal, slender.*
skrike *screech.*
sleen *slay.*
slawe *slew.*
slepen *sleep.*
sly *cunning, sly.*
smal *slender, narrow, slim.*
snowte *muzzle, snout.*
sodeyn *sudden.*
sodeynly *suddenly.*
softe *soft.*
solas *comfort, pleasure, delight.*
somdel *somewhat, rather.*
somtyme *occasionally, sometimes.*
sond *sand.*
sondry *sundry, various.*
sone *son.*
song see **syngen.**
sonne *sun.*
soore *sorely, severely.*
sooth *truth.*
soothfastness *truth.*
soothly *truly, truthfully.*
sorwe *sorrow.*
sorweful *dire, lamentable.*
soverayn *supreme.*
sovereynly *especially, chiefly.*
speche *speech, words.*
speke *speak.*
sprynge *rise, spring up.*
staf *staff.*
stalle *stall, shed.*
stape *advanced.*

stedefast *staunch, fearless, determined.*
sterten *start up.*
stevene *voice.*
stikke *stake, stick.*
stirte see **sterten.**
stonden *stand.*
stoor *store, value.*
strecche *stretch, extend.*
streit *narrow, scanty.*
streite *drawn (as of a sword).*
streyne *compel, constrain.*
stynte *stop, put an end to.*
substance *power to appreciate, ability.*
subtiltee *cunning, cleverness.*
suffisance *contentment.*
suffre *allow, permit.*
superfluitee *excess.*
suspecioun *suspicion.*
suster *sister.*
swerd *sword.*
sweete *charming, delightful.*
swevene *dream.*
swich *such.*
symple *simple, frugal.*
syn *since.*
syngen *sing.*
taak *take.*
tale *tale, heed, account.*
talking *address, discourse.*
tarie *delay, wait.*
techen *direct, guide, teach.*
telle *reckon.*
tercaine *tertian, returning every third day.*
tespye see *espyen.*
that *what, that which.*
that *the great, the notable.*
thee *prosper, succeed.*
thanne *then.*
ther *where, there.*
ther-as *where.*
therewith *in addition, moreover.*
therewithal *moreover, in addition.*
thilke *the same, that same.*
thinken *seem, appear.*

thise *these.*
tho *those.*
thogh *though, although.*
thoughte *thought.*
thre *three.*
thridde *third.*
thritty *thirty.*
throte *throat.*
thurgh *through.*
thyn *thine.*
thynge *thing, circumstance, happening, business.*
tip-toon *tiptoes.*
to *too.*
tomorwe *tomorrow.*
tonyght *last night.*
tool *weapon.*
toold *told.*
toon, toos *toes.*
torment *suffering, pain, agony.*
torne *turn over.*
toun *village.*
touchyng *concerning, with reference to.*
traysoun *treason, treachery.*
trespas *wrong doing, transgression.*
trewe *true, faithful.*
trewely *truly, certainly.*
tribulation *sorrow, trial.*
truste *trust, believe.*
turn *change, check, reverse.*
tweye *two.*
twies *twice.*
tyde *time, hour.*
understonden *understood.*
undertake *guarantee, affirm, assert.*
undiscreet *tactless, indiscreet.*
undren *forenoon, time before midday.*
unto *in addition to.*
up *upon.*
upon *after, in pursuit of.*
upright *flat on his back, face upwards.*
vanitee *emptiness, illusion.*
vengeance *vengeance.*
venym *poison.*

verray *true, very.*
vers *verse, poetry.*
veyn *vain.*
viage *journey, voyage.*
vileynye *wrong, wickedness, unkindness.*
voys *voice.*
waite *watch, lie in wait for.*
war *aware, conscious.*
ware impera., *beware that.*
warnynge *warning, premonition.*
wel *well, carefully, quite.*
wel *happiness, weal.*
wende *go, travel.*
were *was, were.*
werken *cause, work.*
wex *become, grow.*
weylawey *alas.*
whan *when.*
what *what?*
whatso *whatever.*
what that *whatever.*
what though *although.*
wheeras *where.*
wheither *whether.*
whelp *dog, puppy.*
wher *whether.*
wher *where.*
wherfore *for which reason.*
which *who, whom.*
which that *who.*
whilom *once, formerly.*
whit *white.*
whitter *whiter.*
wight *person, man.*
wikke *wicked, evil.*
wilfully *deliberately, intentionally.*
wise *fashion, manner.*
withoute *without, outside.*
witnesse *call as witness.*
wityng *foreknowledge, knowledge.*
wlatsom *loathsome, foul, revolting.*
wo *woe, sorrow, distress.*
wode *wood.*
wol *wish, intend, purpose.*
woltestow contraction for *wilt thou.*
wonder *wondrous, strange* (l. 312);

wonderfully (l. 102).
wone *dwell, live.*
woned *dwelt, lived.*
wonne *won.*
wont *accustomed, used.*
wook *woke.*
woot *know.*
word *word, remark.*
world *world, life, existence.*
wort *cabbage, plant.*
worthy *remarkable, notable, distinguished.*
writ *wrote.*
writen *write.*
wroght *caused, worked.*
wydwe *widow.*
wyf *wife.*
wyn *wine.*
wynke *close the eyes.*
wys *wise.*
wys *certainly.*
wysdom *wisdom.*
yaf *gave.*
ybeen *been.*
ydoon *done.*
ye *yes, yea.*
ye see **eye.**
yeerd *yard, enclosure, garden.*
yelow *yellow.*
yere *year.*
yet *still, even now.*
yeve *give.*
yfounde *found.*
ygon *gone.*
yis *yes, certainly.*
ylogged *lodged.*
ymaginacioun *imagination.*
yn *down, in.*
ynough *enough.*
yolleden *yelled.*
yollen *yell.*
you, yow *you.*
yronne *ran.*
yseyled *sailed.*
ywarned *warned.*
ywis *indeed.*
ywrite *wrote.*

Pan study aids Titles published in the Brodie's Notes series

E. Albee Who's Afraid of Virginia Woolf?

Jane Austen Emma Pride and Prejudice

Anthologies of Poetry: The Metaphysical Poets

Robert Bolt A Man for All Seasons

Harold Brighouse Hobson's Choice

Charlotte Brontë Jane Eyre Villette

Emily Brontë Wuthering Heights

Robert Browning Selected Poetry

Bruce Chatwin On the Black Hill

Geoffrey Chaucer (parallel texts editions) The Nun's Priest's Tale
The Pardoner's Tale The Wife of Bath's Tale

Gerald Cole Gregory's Girl

Daniel Defoe A Journal of the Plague Year

S. Delaney A Taste of Honey

Charles Dickens David Copperfield Great Expectations Oliver Twist

George Eliot Silas Marner

T. S. Eliot Murder in the Cathedal

F. Scott Fitzgerald The Great Gatsby

E. M. Forster A Passage to India

John Fowles The French Lieutenant's Woman

William Golding Lord of the Flies

Graham Greene Brighton Rock

Willis Hall The Long and the Short and the Tall

Thomas Hardy Far from the Madding Crowd
The Mayor of Casterbridge Tess of the d'Urbervilles

Susan Hill I'm the King of the Castle

Barry Hines Kes

James Joyce A Portrait of the Artist as a Young Man

John Keats Selected Poems and Letters of John Keats

D. H. Lawrence Sons and Lovers

Harper Lee To Kill a Mockingbird

Laurie Lee Cider with Rosie

Christopher Marlowe Doctor Faustus

Arthur Miller The Crucible Death of a Salesman

Bill Naughton Spring and Port Wine

Robert C. O'Brien Z for Zachariah

George Orwell Animal Farm 1984

J. B. Priestley An Inspector Calls

J. D. Salinger The Catcher in the Rye

William Shakespeare Antony and Cleopatra As You Like It
Coriolanus Hamlet Julius Caesar King Lear Macbeth
The Merchant of Venice A Midsummer Night's Dream Othello
Romeo and Juliet The Tempest Twelfth Night

G. B. Shaw Pygmalion

John Steinbeck Of Mice and Men & The Pearl

Keith Waterhouse Billy Liar

John Webster The Duchess of Malfi

Tennessee Williams A Streetcar Named Desire and the Glass Menagerie

K. Dowling GCSE: English Coursework – Drama and Poetry

G. Handley and P. Wilkins GCSE: English Coursework – Prose

Pan study aids

The complete guide to GCSE exam success

Authors, highly experienced teachers, examiners and writers in every case, have taken account of ALL syllabuses in their subjects

GCSE Study Aids cover all the essentials, focusing on the areas which carry the most marks and paying particular attention to common points of difficulty

GCSE Study Aids supply expert guidance on how to revise and prepare for the exams

GCSE Study Aids illustrate the varied types of exam questions, explaining exactly what examiners look for

GCSE Study Aids give students the chance to practice their answers using sample questions supplied by the examination boards

Pan study aids

Books in the series: